Passport's Illustrated Guide to
THAILAND

SECOND EDITION

PASSPORT BOOKS
NTC/Contemporary Publishing Group

This edition first published in 2000 by Passport Books
A division of NTC/Contemporary Publishing Group, Inc.
4255 West Touhy Avenue
Lincolnwood (Chicago), Illinois
60712–1975 U.S.A.

Written by Ben Davies

Series adviser: Melissa Shales

The Automobile Association would also like to thank Dinah Eagle of Thomas Cook UK.

© The Automobile Association 1993, 2000.
Maps © The Automobile Association 1993, 2000.

Library of Congress Catalog Card Number: on file

ISBN 0-658-00155-8

All rights reserved. No part of this publication may be reproduced, stored in a retrieval system, or transmitted in any form or by any means, electronic, mechanical, photocopying, recording, or otherwise, without the prior permission of NTC/Contemporary Publishing Group, Inc.

The contents of this publication are believed correct at the time of printing. Nevertheless, the publishers cannot accept responsibility for errors or omissions, or for changes in details given. Assessments of attractions, hotels, restaurants, and so forth are based upon the author's own experience and, therefore, descriptions given in this guide necessarily contain an element of subjective opinion that may not reflect the publishers' opinion or dictate a reader's own experiences on other occasions.

We have tried to ensure accuracy in this guide, but things do change and we would be grateful if readers would advise us of any inaccuracies they may encounter.

Published by Passport Books in conjunction with The Automobile Association and the Thomas Cook Group Ltd.

This book was produced using QuarkXPress™, Aldus Freehand™, and Microsoft Word™ on Apple Macintosh™ computers.

Color separation: BTB Colour Reproduction.

Printed by Edicoes ASA, Oporto, Portugal.

The spelling of place names used on the maps and within the text of this book have been transcribed from the Thai language; consequently slight variations may occur between these name forms and those used locally.

Cover photographs: front, copyright © Rankin Harvey/Dave G. Houser Stock Photography; spine, © Dave G. Houser.

Contents

Introduction	4
History	6
Geography	8
Politics	10
Culture	12
First Steps	14
Walks and Tours	24
What to See	
Bangkok	44
Northern Thailand	74
Northeast Thailand	94
The Eastern Gulf	102
Southern Thailand	110
Getting Away From it All	130
Shopping	138
Entertainment	146
Children	156
Sport	158
Food and Drink	164
Hotels and Accommodation	170
Practical Guide	174
Index and Acknowledgements	191

Walks and Tours

Bangkok's China Town	24
Bangkok's Temples	26
Bangkok's Chao Phraya River	28
Old Thonburi District	30
Bangkok Bars by Night	32
From Bangkok to the River Khwae	34
Chiang Mai's Thaphae Road	36
Chiang Mai's Walled City by Tricycle	38
Circuit of Phuket	40
Cycling Around Sukhothai	42

Maps

Thailand locator	8
Thailand	15
Northern Thailand	16–17
Southern Thailand	23
Bangkok's China Town Walk	24
Bangkok's Temples Tour	26
Bangkok's Chao Phraya River Tour	28
Old Thonburi District Tour	30
From Bangkok to the River Khwae Tour	34
Chiang Mai's Thaphae Road Tour	36
Chiang Mai's Walled City by Tricycle Tour	38
Circuit of Phuket Tour	40
Cycling Around Sukhothai Tour	42
Bangkok	46–7
Chiang Mai	76–7
Phuket	111

Features

The Spirits	18
Buddhism	60
Rice Harvest	70
Hilltribes	84
The People of Issan	98
Royalty	120
Wildlife	134
Markets	144
Go-Go Girl	150

Introduction

Up to 12 hours by plane from Western Europe, four weeks by boat, a world away in spirit, the Kingdom of Thailand remains the quintessence of Eastern promise.

With its chequered rice fields, glittering temples and turquoise seas, it exudes a dreamy unreality. Yet, with its spicy food and crowded cities, it reflects the sheer immediacy of a people living life to the full. Thailand is often called the 'Land of Smiles'.

Here, packed in a country the size of France, are countless worlds: hilltribe people cultivating opium, high-tech industries churning out silicon chips and more than 60 per cent of the population working the fields as they have done for centuries.

From the lush countryside and palm-fringed islands to the polluted capital of Bangkok seems like a million kilometres. But even here, amidst the BMWs, the five-star hotels and chaotic side streets there is little that is conventional, and contrasts abound. What enchants one visitor appals the next and the unexpected is the only norm.

But who can be indifferent to the sight of a Buddhist monk collecting alms from a layman or a hilltribe woman buying kebabs in the market? Who, too, can imagine the exhaust fumes of a million cars, the smell of a million flowers and the calm of a temple *wat* surrounded by gilded Buddhas? Thailand is visually spectacular.

A beautiful southern beach – Kata Noi

INTRODUCTION

Thailand is no longer the undiscovered paradise of yesteryear. But with its 25 million rice farmers, its king and its religion of compromise, the kingdom still offers visitors the feel of the East tinged with the comforts of the West along with the excitement, the frustrations and the feel of somewhere many worlds away. Sometimes colourful, sometimes chaotic, Thailand has managed to remain always uniquely itself.

THAILAND QUOTES

'The men are black, the zone is hot and the inhabitants much given to pleasure and ryot.'
Samuel Purchas, early 17th-century explorer

'It makes you laugh with delight to think that anything so fantastic could exist on this sombre earth. They are gorgeous; they glitter with gold and whitewash, yet are not garish.'
Somerset Maugham

'The streets, stretching out of sight, are alleys of clear running water. The horizon is tall trees, above which are visible the sparkling towers and pyramids of the pagodas. Certainly, I myself have never seen lovelier.'
Abbé de Choisy

Mae Sot, in the far north near the Burmese border

'This Kingdom is good. In the water there are fish, in the fields there is rice. The ruler does not levy taxes ... the faces of the people are happy.'
13th-century stone inscription found in Sukhothai

> The spelling of place names used on the maps and within the text of this book have been transcribed from the Thai language; consequently slight variations may occur between these name forms and those used locally.

Left: Wat Phra Kaeo, the royal chapel inside the Grand Palace, Bangkok

History

3500 BC
Traces of an early Bronze Age civilisation discovered in Ban Chiang, northeast Thailand.
8th–11th century AD
Arrival of the Mons and Khmers from Cambodia.
10th–12th century
Thais migrate from China into northern Thailand, displacing the Khmers.
1238
Foundation of Sukhothai, in the period known as the 'Dawn of Happiness', the first independent Thai kingdom.
1279–98
Reign of King Ramkhamhaeng (Rama the Brave), one of the great early monarchs.
1350
Founding of Ayutthaya.
1378
Sukhothai becomes a vassal state of neighbouring Ayutthaya, a powerful Thai kingdom to the south.
1390–1431
Ayutthaya expands to include Chiang Mai and parts of Cambodia.
1600–88
Highpoint of Ayutthaya. The Court receives emissaries from France, Portugal, Holland and Britain.
1656–88
Reign of King Narai. Thai ambassadors sent to the Court of Louis XIV.
1767
Conquest and destruction of Ayutthaya by the Burmese. All but 10,000 of the inhabitants are killed or taken into slavery and the city is laid to waste.
1768
General Taksin drives out the Burmese and moves the capital to Thonburi.
1782
Taksin goes insane and is executed by being beaten to death with a scented sandalwood club.
1782–1809
Reign of Rama I, the first king of the great Chakri dynasty. A new capital is declared in Bangkok.
1809–24
Reign of Rama II.
1824–51
Reign of Rama III, the king renowned for piously embracing Buddhism.
1851–68
Reign of Rama IV, known as King Mongkut, one of the great reformers of the 19th century and the ruler depicted in the film *The King and I*.
1855–8
Trade treaties signed with Britain, France and the United States.
1868–1910
Reign of Rama V, known as King Chulalongkorn, the man credited with bringing Thailand into the modern world.
1910–25
Reign of Oxford-educated Rama VI, known as King Vajiravudh.
1925
Beginning of the reign of Eton-educated Rama VII, known as King Prajadhipok.
1932
First in a long line of coups by the military. Rama VII steps aside and a constitutional monarchy is declared.
1935–46
Reign of Rama VIII, the child king who was mysteriously found shot in bed. The enigma of the death has yet to be solved.
1941
Japanese occupation of Thailand with

HISTORY

Revered Thai monarchs: Taksin, Rama VI and Rama VIII

the compliance of the Thai government. Opposition groups operate underground.
1946
Reign of Rama IX, known as King Bhumiphol Adulyadej, best loved of the Chakri monarchs.
1965
The Thais remain ostensibly neutral in the Vietnam war but allow US bases on Thai soil.
1973
Students take to the streets of Bangkok in protest against the military. More than 200 are killed or wounded.
1975
Saigon falls to the Vietcong and the last US troops fly out of Vietnam.
1976
A further coup sparked off by a violent confrontation between police and students. The army seizes control.
1981
Abortive coup attempt by a group of army officers known as the 'Young Turks'.

1988
Advent of democratically elected government and the beginning of an unprecedented boom.
1991
The 17th coup brings to an end the Chatichai administration on the grounds of corruption.
1991–2
Military caretaker government, under Prime Minister Anand.
March 1992
General Suchinda appointed Prime Minister.
May 1992
Pro-democracy protestors shot down by troops in Bangkok.
September 1992
Democracy survives under Chuan Leekpai's long-lasting government.
July 1995
Chart Thai party is elected amid growing cynicism about political corruption.
1996
50th anniversary of King Bhumipol's reign. New Aspiration Party elected, led by Chaovalit Yong Chaiyudh.

Geography

The Kingdom of Thailand lies just south of the Tropic of Cancer, some 9,485km from London or Paris and some 7,495km from Sydney. Thailand is part of the vast area known as Indo-China which contains the neighbouring countries of Laos, Cambodia and Burma.

Formed millions of years ago, the Indo-Chinese landmass was reshaped over the centuries by earthquakes and volcanic activity that created the fairy-tale rock formations at Phang Nga as well as the magnificent limestone ridges of the northern hills.

These same geological processes gave the kingdom its irregular shape, which the local people compare to an elephant's head. To the north is the rounded skull, towards Korat in the east is the protruding ear and Bangkok is located at the elephant's mouth. To the south the trunk extends all the way down to the border with Malaysia.

Undreamt of variety
Thailand is a delightfully varied country. Parts of its extensive coastline would be the envy of any tropical island paradise, whilst the coastal plains, rain forests, lush valleys and dramatic mountains only add to the scenic variety.

You will not find snow here, however. Thailand's highest point is only 2,565m above sea level at Doi Inthanon near Chiang Mai in the northern region. Though high hills continue down the west part of the country, following the Burmese border down to the coast of Malaysia, they cannot match their Himalayan parentage.

On the other hand, Thailand does have plains in vast quantity, rich fertile tracts of land that have made the country one of the most productive rice growers in the world – harvesting more than 20 million tonnes every year. These plains are irrigated by the great rivers of the Ping, the Yom and the Nan which snake down from the north to the town of Nakhon Sawan, where they merge to form the great Chao Phraya river, known as the 'Mother of Waters'.

The Mekong river also cuts through the arid chain of land that lies to the northeast, formed by the Korat plateau, which extends through the poorest part of the country.

The Mekong River

Almost midway down the landmass, the kingdom narrows. The Tenasserim and Phuket hills, an important source of tin, lie down the western coast leaving room on the east coast for rubber and coconut plantations and the endless beaches that have become the gems in Thailand's tourist crown.

Vital statistics

With 76 provinces and a landmass the size of France, Thailand still manages to come out with some fairly disparate statistics. The distance from the northern tip to the southern tip is 1,700km and from the arid plains of Korat to the border with Burma is 800km. Below the centre of the Kingdom, southwards, the land narrows to as little as 16km – indeed so small a distance that on clear days it is possible to look from one coast to the other.

Of the total landmass, 60 per cent is under plantations, mainly of rice, rubber and tapioca, products that have made Thailand one of the biggest agricultural producers in the world. A further 20 per cent is under forest, a figure that has fallen rapidly since the days when much of the countryside was a mass of jungle, but which is still enough to conserve vast areas of teak and pine. Even the two coastlines are different, the one green and tropical, the other characterised by hills and limestone formations.

Given this variety, it is hardly surprising that visitors can come back to Thailand year after year, visiting each different town and region, and every time discovering yet another country.

Politics

*I*n the merry-go-round life in Thailand, politics plays one of the most visible – and yet least important – features. Seventeen coups have shaped the face of the kingdom, while more than 20 constitutions and prime ministers have shown the vulnerability of the political game and the enduring power of the military.

Indeed, until the early 20th century, politics was an irrelevance and the monarchy the all-pervading power. For the four centuries prior to that, subjects who even so much as looked at the monarch could have had their heads chopped off.

Thailand is now a constitutional monarchy and the people more politically aware

Although change began with the great Chakri kings – and especially with Rama V (1868–1910) who ended the ancient custom of prostration – the real death knell only came in 1932 when the military took power and the absolute monarchy was abolished.

Since then the pendulum has swung from the military back to democracy and back again to the military.

Yet for all the turbulence and the colourful rhetoric, Thailand has managed to avoid the civil wars that have torn neighbouring Cambodia, Laos and Vietnam, and in so doing has paradoxically established itself as one of the most stable and loyal members of the non-communist world as well as a leading voice in ASEAN, the Association of South East Asian Nations.

The decades of unrest

If it were not for the first military coup of 1932, the king might still have held sway. But the coup brought an end to the constitutional monarchy, changing the pattern of politics for good and ushering in a period of uncertainty.

During subsequent decades Thailand withstood the winds of change that were reshaping Indo-China, but the Vietnam

War, and the consequent influx of Americans, once again led to the declaration of martial law. When students took to the streets to demonstrate against the military the tanks were sent in and hundreds of students were killed or wounded.

In the aftermath, the military leaders were forced to step down, a new coalition government took power and for a period of three years the status quo remained intact.

Since then, the political theatricalities have continued, although, with the exception of the early 1990s, violence has been almost entirely absent.

It is little surprise that the Thais regard the whole business of politics with humour. The constant flux keeps people intrigued, but rarely does it change things. Bangkok residents complain that the wrong government gets in whoever they vote for. To foreigners this is a sign of instability, but to the Thais it is just a sign of life and a reflection of the theatrical nature of the people themselves.

A signboard advertises a political satire, in the form of a puppet shadow-play

Taste of democracy

Even today, democracy is a strange word to the Thais. Democracy may have given a voice to the nation, a vote to the people, but rampant vote-buying has put paid to any true ideal, whilst to the average farmer, it is largely irrelevant compared to the rains and the harvest.

Constitutionally, however, the country is governed by a cabinet and a national assembly supported by a highly educated civil service. Moving down the parliamentary pyramid are the 76 provinces each with a governor and a provincial capital. And at the bottom, there are hundreds of thousands of village councils.

For all that, control of the purse strings and the people means that the military is never far from power. They still have their own investment funds, their own political alliances, even their own bank.

In future that position may change as prosperity spreads and the threat of communism – and the fear of Vietnam, Burma and Laos – is finally laid to rest. But as the 1992 shootings in Bangkok demonstrated when hundreds of pro-democracy protestors were killed or wounded by soldiers, the military remains a critical force – and politics an unpredictable and for the great majority a largely irrelevant matter.

Culture

*A*ll the colour and all the exotic arts of the East are to be found in Thailand. Whether classical dancing, an arrangement of jasmine flowers or a temple mural, the country excels in its artistic achievements. Nor is this merely a show of Eastern convention, but one of the clearest examples of the people's love of colour and of life.

The most famous monument in all Thailand, the Grand Palace in Bangkok, is in many ways the synthesis of all these – with its clutch of gilded and glistening spires, its murals of the *Ramayana,* and the revered temple of the Emerald Buddha.

But if you miss the Grand Palace there are plenty of other examples. Indeed, some estimates put the number of temples at 26,000 and Buddha images at five million, about one for every dozen members of the population.

The invisible force

Pervading everything in Thailand is Buddhism, the 'middle way' and the religion of 90 per cent of the people.

That religion came 1,200 years ago from India, brought by missionaries from the Emperor Ashoka, and its influence has spawned not only the people, but also the art that they produced.

Religious writings of the time provided strict rules for creating any image of the Buddha, which was to have 32 primary features and 80 secondary ones. Even so, Thai artists left their own indelible marks as a reflection of the age in which they lived.

Early styles show the broad rugged features of the Buddha with bulging eyes, often in the position of subduing Mara, the symbol of all evil.

During the 13th and 14th centuries, the Buddhas became more serene, the features less pronounced, leading to the famous Sukhothai Buddha, the highpoint of Thai art. Later periods could not match such artistic heights and the art of the Bangkok period (late 17th century onwards) degenerated into the production of ornate, heavy handed royal figures.

Various other influences have also moulded the kingdom throughout its long history including Indian mythology and the art of the early Khmer and Mon civilisations. These too have been absorbed and reworked into something unique, something quintessentially Thai.

The solid gold Buddha of Wat Traimit

A wealth of *wats*

A *wat* is a temple in Thailand. But a *wat* is also a communal home for the monks, a gathering point for the village and, traditionally, even a school.

Originally they were simple structures made of wood and found in every rural commune. Later temples were built specifically to contain relics of the Buddha himself. The most important *wats* are called *pra that* or *wat mahathat* and are supported by royalty. Others are funded by the people themselves who give money in order to win merit and secure themselves a better life in the next earthly cycle.

Going for a song

Classical music to the Thais is as sweet as to the Western ear. But it has no harmonic value, no regular rhythm and

Wat Phra Kaeo, the most dazzling of all Thailand's glittering temples

even uses different notes to those of the Western scale.

Originally the sounds were used to accompany dances developed for kings and played for royalty. In later years, classical music found its way into local festivals where a *piphat* orchestra, comprising 15 to 20 members, banged gongs called *gong wong yai* or played the Thai xylophone known as the *ranad*.

These days the place to hear classical music is in tourist restaurants or, if you are lucky, the National Theatre. But do not expect to hear it outside these establishments. Thai pop music now takes precedence and it is that that you are likely to hear everywhere, throughout the country.

First Steps

*E*veryone visiting Thailand is struck by the relative ease of getting around and the openness of the people with whom they come into contact. Trains run on time, white towels are offered for washing your brows and even the tourist police speak English (most of the time) and smile. The Thais are known for their good manners.

The initial impression of Westernisation is almost misleading. Like any Asian country, Thailand has its own unique customs; while many are merely a matter of courtesy, others are so deep set that they fill the visitor with wonder. It is no coincidence that the Thais call foreigners *farangs*, meaning 'aliens'.

Below is a touchlist of things to remember. Thais are tolerant people, but it is best to try and fit in.

This young lady is demonstrating the *wai*, the traditional Thai greeting; the higher the hands, the more respectful the salutation

Culture shock

If your first stop is Bangkok, prepare for that wonderous experience known as culture shock and commonly composed of heat, lead pollution and dismay. To survive the maelstrom on the senses, reduce initial hassles to a minimum: make sure you have a hotel reservation, take a taxi from the airport, buy a map and refuse all touts.

If you are arriving after a long-haul flight, take things easily to begin with. Drink lots of water and go easy on sunbathing. Most doctors advise sleep. Better still, find a spot near the river to sit and absorb the calm and the chaos.

The next day get up early, before the traffic, and explore the sights and sounds. Leave your preconceived notions behind and remember that the Thai religion of impermanence negates the need to hurry. In Thailand life goes at its own speed: in Bangkok at a chaotic rate and in the rice fields and government offices at a slow ebb. Nothing a tourist can do will change that. The only way to handle it is to be as the Buddhists and accept.

FIRST STEPS

Entering the spirit of the place
Thais are a fun-loving race. As such they want everyone else to have fun when they are in Thailand. To join the party you generally do not have to go far. People come up to talk to you or to drink with you. Often they want to know about your family, if you are married and how much money you earn.

Do not be put out by such questions. If you do not want to answer them then be evasive. Always beware of those who try to befriend you for other reasons. Tourism is not new and there are always those who prey on tourists for what they can get – be it free meals or money for tours. Treat people with courtesy, but never lower your guard completely.

Thais are always neatly dressed, like this girl in her formal attire

Greetings
The traditional Thai greeting, known as the *wai*, is a gracefully fluent movement that is still commonly used. To do it, hold the palms of your hands together and bring them up to your chin. Bend forward lowering the head. Traditionally the more important the person, the lower you bend.

Thais generally greet one another thus, but foreigners mainly with handshakes. Even so, it can do no harm to learn the Thai way.

Linguistic nuances

Thai is a complex language. It is tonal, and has 44 consonants and 38 vowels. Given time constraints, most visitors get little opportunity to practise going native. For those who would like to try, however, it is still worth investing a few hours prior to departure in learning a few of the essentials.

Try, with the help of a phrase book, to master a few basic words and always remember that at the end of every phrase, males say *krap* and females say *ka*. The Thais are extremely polite and any attempt at learning their language will be greatly appreciated.

The proverbial smile

The Thai smile: there is no other hallmark that is quite so endemic. But, like many such 'Thaisms', it can conceal a host of meanings. Thais smile because they are happy. They smile because they are embarrassed. Some smile because it makes them money. Accept their smiles and try to reciprocate, but never jump to conclusions about their meaning.

In the same way, Thais rarely show anger. When they do, it is with uncharacteristic vigour. Never argue excessively and if you are angry smile and leave. Thais do this and, for the most part, it seems to work.

The Thai smile, Rayong-style

THE SPIRITS

On the top of almost every post, or situated outside almost any building, is a miniature house or temple known as the *chao thai*. This normally contains joss sticks, rice and water: it often has beds and accommodates the most important single resident of the house: the *phra phum* or lord of the place. Here people make daily offerings of food, flowers, incense and candles.

Spirits not only live in the towns and cities of Thailand, but also in the trees, in the hills, in the winds and in the rain.

They are believed to be the biggest determinants of good fortune and, if not treated properly and with the proper deference due them, the reason for bad luck.

Farmers hoping for a good harvest, young girls looking for a suitable husband or gamblers hoping to win a lottery: none can afford to ignore them.

When a new office block is to be built, the spirit house will be the first thing to be planned. And when a tree is cut down, a special ceremony will be held to appease the misplaced spirit within.

In the far north of the country, many of the tribespeople hold offerings to the 'grandmother of the crops', while in the south the local fishermen erect phalluses pointing out to sea to fertilise the water.

Some Thais no longer believe everything they are told about the spirits. The Thais are a practical people, however, and – just in case it is true – almost everyone will make offerings in the hope that it will do them good.

Spirit houses come in all shapes and sizes, as do the offerings left there

FIRST STEPS

Monks walk everywhere, as personal motorised transport is forbidden

Purchasing power
Unless in doubt, bargain. That is the magic rule. It applies in shops, in markets, in taxis and occasionally even in travel agents. The art of bargaining is to decide how much you are prepared to pay for a given product or service beforehand and if possible to get it cheaper.

The way it works is this. You see a lurid green lacquerware pot which you can imagine in your home. Ask how much it is (*taurai?* in Thai). As a rule the salesman will quote you a price 30 to 50 per cent too high. You must say 'too expensive' (*peng pai*) and quote a price 20 per cent lower than you believe the lacquer pot is worth. The salesman will then, in all likelihood, lower his original price and you in turn should increase yours, but never above your orginal target.

At this point the salesman may well tell you that he cannot make money, that he has 20 children to feed and a blind mother-in-law. Smile, but look unimpressed, finger through some different articles and put in a final offer. If he accepts, you are obliged to pay up: if not move on and start again.

If you cannot speak Thai, use each finger to denote 10 *baht*. Many shops now use calculators, keying in their own price, then allowing you to put in yours before coming out with a compromise.

Tackling the tout
From the moment you arrive in Thailand you will become the centre of adulation for a strange breed of individual known as the tout. Touts dress smartly, generally speak good English and make their money by persuading you to go on special tours, by acting as your private guide and by taking you on shopping trips.

You are strongly advised to resist their attentions. Touts are outlawed. They may be friendly but they may cost you an arm and a leg. If you are in doubt, ask advice at your hotel or at the tourist office.

Taxis and *tuk tuks*

One of the first things you will be confronted with on arrival is a three-wheeled, unsightly, smelly motorbike taxi. This contraption is known as a *tuk tuk*. It is Thailand's favourite and fastest means of city transport. *Tuk tuks* are relatively cheap, are available at almost any hour and are generally safe.

To get a *tuk tuk* all you need to do is wave one down. Tell the driver where you want to go and agree a price before you get in (you must bargain).

Always sympathetic to other needs, Bangkok and the main cities also offer an abundance of conventional taxis, *songthaews* (pick-up trucks) and three-wheeled pedal bikes. Whichever mode of transport you take, make sure you fix a price before you leave (see **Public Transport** on page 188).

The Three Pillars

In the Thai mentality, three bastions rise above all others: the king, Buddhism and the nation. Never speak against them or question them unduly.

Monks, especially, should be regarded as sacrosanct. Women should not touch them, nor pass anything directly to them. Especial care should be taken on crowded buses. Similarly never take liberties with the royal family. Even today, despite tremendous strides towards Westernisation and the gradual erosion of certain values (you often see monks smoking), the people take a fiercely patriotic line.

What to wear

Thais dress neatly. Whether rich or poor, from the city or the country, they take great pains on how they present themselves, believing that appearance reflects status. Foreigners are not expected to follow suit, but they are expected to show a little respect. Topless sunbathing is widespread on almost all the main tourist beaches, but it is still widely looked down upon by the local inhabitants. Jackets and ties may not be common requirements, yet in the really exclusive hotel restaurants, they are appreciated.

When visiting *wats* make sure that you look presentable (no shorts or sleeveless tops should be worn). And when entering people's homes, always remember to take off your shoes.

A tourist poses with girls in national dress at the Rose Garden

Exploring the countryside

Once you have got your feet firmly on Thai soil, the next step is to organise an itinerary. This is the easiest part. Thailand has a vast choice of sights and countless tour agencies to arrange your visits to them.

Most visitors will want to spend a few days in the capital, Bangkok, exploring the markets, canals and temples. During this time you can acclimatise, book tickets and arrange the remainder of your holiday.

Many destinations are now accessible by air, others by train and bus. Do not, however, make the mistake of trying to fit everything into a two-week trip. Air travel may make the trip physically possible but delays and hassles will make it more trouble than it is worth.

The mountainous north

The north is where the mountains and hilltribes are to be found. This is the most popular region for visitors, with Chiang Mai – the capital – playing host to top-class hotels and endless numbers of guest houses. People come here to go trekking or to explore the 'Golden Triangle' and the delightful charms of Lanna, the old Thai kingdom that flourished centuries ago.

The arid plains of the northeast

The northeast is an area of vast arid plains stretching to the Cambodian and Laotian borders. Few tourists visit it, yet the region contains beautiful old Khmer ruins and retains the feel of traditional Thailand, with its plodding water buffalo and poor rural communities. Issan, the Thai name for this region, is for those who want to get away from it all, who have more time and fewer expectations and who preferably speak a few words of the language. Sights are a considerable distance apart and are mainly situated out of town. Private transport is a definite advantage.

The Gulf of Thailand

The strip of land known as the Gulf (southeast of Bangkok) offers the closest beaches to the capital. Originally it sprang up around Pattaya, but it now extends all the way from Bang Saen to Rayong. For those who have less time or who want a weekend break, it has good swimming as well as the beautiful island of Ko Samet: further afield is Ko Chang island and the inland Southern Beaches.

For those in search of beaches and islands, the south is the region to come to. It comprises some 2,080km of coastline, washed by balmy seas, as well as coral reefs and delicious seafoods. Some islands – like Phuket and, increasingly, Ko Samui – have become international destinations with five-star hotels. Others, like Krabi, offer a taste of relatively unspoilt beach paradise with a variety of accommodation.

Khmer ruins, Cambodia

FIRST STEPS

Walk around Bangkok's China Town

A walk around one of Bangkok's busiest market areas, home to some of the city's most congested streets and numerous sprawling wooden houses.
Allow 2 hours.

Start at Tha Ratchawong pier (easily reached by express boat). Take the nearest exit and walk down the long wide strip known as Ratchawong Road which heads due north.

1 RATCHAWONG ROAD
Although no longer the strict preserve of the Chinese, Ratchawong remains very much their traditional heartland, with its old banks, trading branches and shuttered wooden houses. To the right and left are little alleyways selling hardware and textiles. Some stalls even sell bird's nest soup believed to boost longevity and libido.
Walk along Ratchawong Road for 450m and take the small road to your right signposted Soi Wanit 1, formerly known as Sampeng Lane.

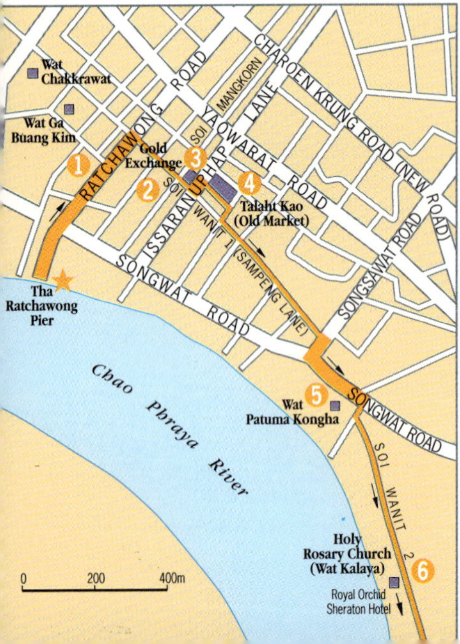

2 SAMPENG LANE
Once a maze of alleys containing opium dens and gambling parlours, the famous Sampeng Lane has mellowed in recent years but remains one of the most fascinating and congested areas of the city. Many little side streets specialise in lanterns, others in herbal remedies. Watch out, too, for the little *kong tek* shops where houses and cars made of paper are burnt by the Chinese in order to send them to the spirit world of deceased relatives.
Continue down Soi Wanit 1 until you reach the first main intersection, with Soi Mangkorn, where you will see the old Gold Exchange.

3 GOLD EXCHANGE

Of all the buildings along Sampeng Lane, this is one of the most distinguished, with its lovely old façade, its shabby balconies and its faded air of grandeur. At one time this was the centre for all gold trading. Today, like many shops in China Town it continues to stock gold bracelets and earrings, carefully weighed out on an ancient pair of scales.

Continue along Soi Wanit 1, past the Gold Exchange; at the next crossing turn left down Issaranuphap Lane, then first right down a small alley into Talaht Kao.

4 TALAHT KAO (OLD MARKET)

You can smell Talaht Kao before you ever see it – a nauseous odour of dried fish, squid and prawns piled up in great wicker baskets along the alleyway. This is one of the oldest and most pungent of Bangkok's Chinese markets, but it is strictly for the curious. Purchasers eat at their own risk.

Continue to the end of the alley then turn right back on to Soi Wanit 1. At this point you leave the narrow congested streets behind. Keep walking for 400m past the little old houses with wooden shutters and further on past the gem shops. When you reach the end of the road, continue almost straight over on to Songwat Road. Wat Patuma Kongha is on the right.

5 WAT PATUMA KONGHA

A former execution site for royal criminals, Wat Patuma Kongha has since gone through something of a metamorphosis. Inside the courtyard you will find rows of golden Buddhas and a haven of calm. Yet it was only in the mid-19th century, during the reign of Rama IV, known as King Mongkut, that the last royal victim, a cousin of the king, was beaten to death with a club.

Leave Wat Patuma Kongha and continue down Songwat Road for 100m, then turn right down Soi Phanit Rang Si. This curves left into Soi Wanit 2 which, after 700m will bring you to Wat Kalaya, known as the Holy Rosary Church.

Many shops in China Town specialise in gold items

6 HOLY ROSARY CHURCH (WAT KALAYA)

Originally constructed by Portuguese Catholics who fled from Ayutthaya to Thonburi after the city fell in 1767, Wat Kalaya has since been totally rebuilt. It remains an incongruous sight. Inside is a wooden pulpit along with stained-glass windows depicting episodes from the Old and New Testaments. There are even daily services in Thai or Chinese.

Leave the Rosary Church and continue down Soi Wanit 2 until you reach the Royal Orchid Sheraton Hotel. From there you can catch an express boat or a taxi home.

TOUR

Bangkok's Temples

This walking tour takes in some of the most famous and most beautiful of Bangkok's 400 temples as well as providing glimpses of markets, waterways and famous landmarks. *Allow 3 hours.*

Take a taxi or tuk tuk *to the Oriental Hotel off Charoen Krung Road on the banks of the Chao Phraya river.*

1 ORIENTAL HOTEL
Built nearly 115 years ago, the Oriental has become one of the best-known hotels in Asia. Joseph Conrad and Graham Greene both resided here, as did Somerset Maugham, who nearly died of malaria. If you are dresssed with sufficient propriety (ie no flip-flops or vest tops) wander into the authors' lounge where you can see some of the old-worldly magic still at work.
Leave the hotel and turn right to the Oriental pier. Catch one of the Chao Phraya express boats plying upriver (to the right) and ask for Tha Rachini, the landing for Pak Khlong Market. Alight here.

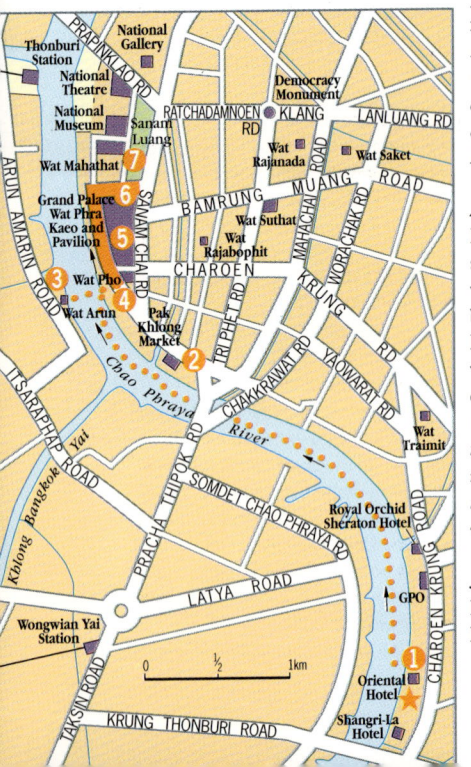

2 PAK KHLONG MARKET
Bangkok's biggest wholesale market is a sensory delight of orchids, cabbages, wriggling frogs and chillies freshly brought in from the provinces by boat. Explore the little alleyways with their old wooden houses and treat yourself to an exotic fruit sold at the sidestalls.
Wander back to Tha Rachini pier and catch the express boat to Tha Thien pier just a few minutes further upriver. Get off and take the tiny baht boat to the temple of Wat Arun, which lies directly opposite.

3 WAT ARUN
Formerly used as the royal temple by King Taksin of Thonburi, Wat Arun lost

some of its royal notoriety when the insane monarch was bludgeoned to death with a sandalwood club. But the temple, with its 104m spire, remains one of Bangkok's best-known landmarks and is covered in porcelain donated by loyal Chinese residents. At the back, wander among the old monks' quarters with their wooden dwellings and the feel of rural Thailand. Note the beautiful lacquerware designs on the door of the temple.
Cross back over the river to Tha Thien pier. Exit through the gate, and turn right along the outer walls of Wat Pho. The entrance is on your left.

4 WAT PHO
Famed for its vast reclining Buddha which is 45m long and has mother-of-pearl inlaid feet, Wat Pho also contains more than 100 *chedis,* (spire-like pagodas), a herbal clinic and a school of traditional massage. The *wat* was originally built in the 16th century and has since been restored to its original glory. On the way out, have your fortune read by an astrologer.
Leave Wat Pho, turn right and walk 800m alongside the massive white walls of the Grand Palace until you reach the entrance.

5 GRAND PALACE
Built by King Rama I, and extended and ennobled by his successors, the Grand Palace is one of the most important sights in Bangkok, containing enough to occupy anyone for a day (see page 50). A brief tour can be taken of the main buildings and of the famous Wat Phra Kaeo, the Temple of the Emerald Buddha.
On the way out, pass the ticket counter and turn immediately to the right for the Royal Thai Decorations and Coin Pavilion.

Wat Pho, probably Bangkok's oldest temple

6 ROYAL THAI DECORATIONS AND COIN PAVILION
Inside the pavilion is a magnificent collection of ceramic coins and silver money used from the early 11th century. Wander upstairs to see a selection of royal crowns, jewelled swords, brocaded robes and objects carved from betel-nut.
Leave the museum and the Grand Palace, turn right and, almost directly opposite, you will see the vast open green known as Sanam Luang.

7 SANAM LUANG
A former cremation ground for kings and the place where the weekend market used to be held, Sanam Luang is also the spot where the early Chakri monarchs used to exercise their white elephants. Today the grounds are popular with walkers, kite-flyers and those selling snacks of kebabs and fried grasshoppers.
From Sanam Luang, catch a taxi or tuk tuk *home or take an express boat from the Tha Chang pier opposite the Grand Palace.*

Bangkok's Chao Phraya River

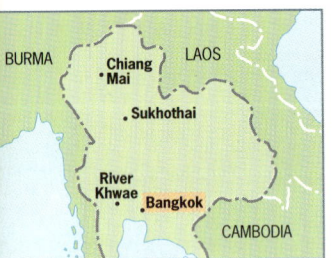

This delightful river trip provides views of city life and of some fine monuments. *Allow 2 hours.*

Start at Wat Rajsingkorn pier on Charoen Krung Road, near the Menam Hotel. Catch a Chao Phraya express boat heading upstream (to the right) and ask for Krung Thon Bridge. After passing Taksin Bridge you will see the Old Customs House on your right, just past the Oriental Hotel.

Nearby

Grand Palace

National Museum

Wat Mahathat

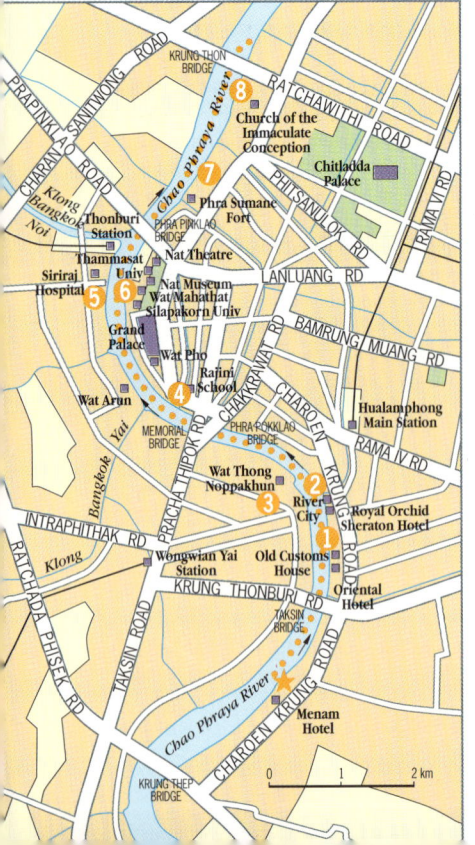

1 OLD CUSTOMS HOUSE

Built in the late 19th century, this delightful old building hugging the river bank was once the main customs house for Bangkok. Although still sporting louvered shutters, it is now used by the city's fire brigade. The building does, however, give an idea of what the whole riverfront may once have looked like.

From the Old Customs House, the boat passes the Royal Orchid Sheraton Hotel. Next door is River City.

2 RIVER CITY

The first of several modern shopping centres on the river, and a three-storey haven for antique explorers, River City bustles with silk shops, ancient elephants from Laos and rare pieces from Cambodia. On the first Sunday of every month there is even an auction.

Beyond River City on the left you will glimpse the outline of Wat Thong Noppakhun.

3 WAT THONG NOPPAKHUN

Even the Buddhists can see the humorous side of life. Until the mid-19th century Wat Thong Noppakhun was distinguished by murals of urinating angels and others showing their bare buttocks. King Rama IV was horrified and had the controversial paintings retouched.

Further upriver from Wat Thong Noppakhun, you will see the Rajini School on the right bank after Memorial Bridge.

4 RAJINI SCHOOL

The neo-classical building that contains the Rajini School was founded in 1904 by Queen Saowapa Pongsri to educate the young women of the time. Although something of a revolutionary concept (until then only boys were considered worthy of education), the school went on to become one of Thailand's most pre-eminent academic establishments.

From the Rajini School, the boat passes the Wat Arun (on the left) and the Grand Palace (on the right). Further down on the left bank is the modern white façade of the Siriraj Hospital.

5 SIRIRAJ HOSPITAL

Ordinary it may look from the outside, but the Siriraj Hospital museum contains some unusual specimens, including foetuses, the skulls of electrocuted criminals and the body of the most notorious criminal of the lot: Si Oui, the Chinese mass-murderer who strangled seven children and, for his sins, is now preserved in formaldehyde.

Beyond Siriraj Hospital, on the right bank, is Thammasat University.

6 THAMMASAT UNIVERSITY

Founded just before World War II, Thammasat is a radical educational institution. During student uprisings in 1973 and 1976 protesting against military influence, army leaders sent in tanks and helicopters and many people were killed or injured, paving the way for a new constitution.

After passing Phra Pinklao Bridge, you will see the Phra Sumane Fort on your right.

Thammasat University specialises in law, economics and politics

7 PHRA SUMANE FORT

The octagonal fort which looms over the river was originally built in the late 18th century, during the reign of King Rama I, as a defence against invaders. The present structure, however, only dates from Bangkok's bicentennial (1982).

Shortly before you arrive at the next bridge (Krung Thon Bridge) you will see the Church of the Immaculate Conception on the right.

8 CHURCH OF THE IMMACULATE CONCEPTION

Built around 1674 by Father Louis Laneau, the church served as the religious centre for Portuguese Catholics. The church was rebuilt in 1837 and contains beautiful imported windows and statues of the Virgin.

After passing under the next bridge either alight at Sang Hee pier and catch an express boat back or continue to Nonthaburi, the bustling little market town which lies 30 minutes further upriver. Be warned, however: the last boat back leaves Nonthaburi at 6pm.

Old Thonburi District

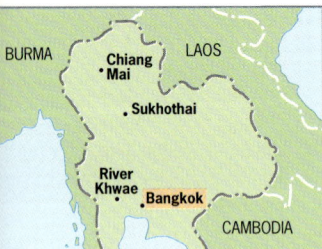

This is one of the least-visited areas of town with glimpses of the old Bangkok and the chance to wander a little more adventurously away from the crowds. *Allow 2 hours.*

Begin at the Tha Saphan Phut express boat landing at the foot of Memorial Bridge and catch the baht ferry that crosses the Chao Phraya river to Pracha Thipok Road on the opposite bank.

1 MEMORIAL BRIDGE (PHRA BUDDHA YOTFA BRIDGE)

King Rama VII opened this first bridge across the Chao Phraya river on 6 April, 1932. Two months later a revolution forced the king to give up absolute rule in Thailand. Memorial Bridge is one of seven in the city crossing the Chao Phraya and connecting Bangkok to Thailand's former capital, Thonburi. *Disembark on the far side of the river. Follow Pracha Thipok Road for about 100m until you see Wat Prayoonwong on the corner of Thetsaban 1 Road.*

2 WAT PRAYOONWONG

Known as the 'Turtle Temple', Wat Prayoonwong contains vast numbers of these floating reptiles fed with papaya and sliced bananas by people who wish to win merit and secure themselves a better life in the next earthly cycle. The temple

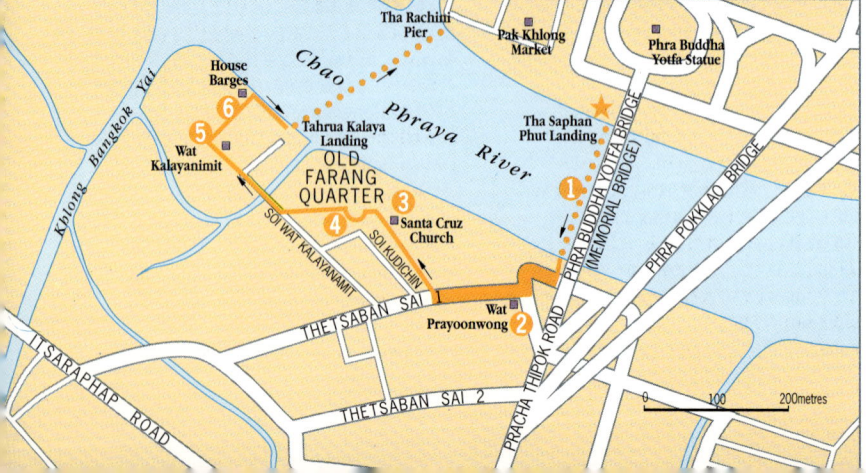

was built in the reign of King Rama III by a member of Thailand's powerful Bunnag family and is especially noted for its fine doors decorated with mother-of-pearl.

Leave the temple and walk down Thetsaban 1 for about 200m until you glimpse a church tower on your right. To get to Santa Cruz Church you must cross through the graveyard which also irreverently doubles up as a car park.

3 SANTA CRUZ CHURCH

One of the most delightful of the old buildings on the river bank, Santa Cruz Church stands on the site of an earlier and even more magnificent edifice. The original church was built more than 200 years ago by a collection of Portuguese adventurers, traders and missionaries, but was torn down in 1913 to make way for the new. Note the graveyard where the former residents have been interred in concrete lockers, each of the deceased identified by a photograph. Visitors will find this old Portuguese section of the city around the church a quiet oasis, far from the hustle and bustle of modern-day Bangkok.

Leave the church and continue west along the narrow walkways that run parallel to the river. You will soon enter the district known as the Old Farang Quarter.

4 OLD FARANG QUARTER

At the turn of the century, the area around Santa Cruz Church was still popular with foreigners, known as *farangs* in Thai, who resided in spacious villas within easy boating distance of China Town and the Grand Palace. Though the *farangs* and most of the villas are gone, you can still see some charming old wooden houses, closely packed in a network of interconnecting *sois* (alleys).

Nobody seems to hurry here; it is as if the world has left this piece of Bangkok behind.

Aiming to keep parallel to the river, follow one of the narrow walkways that snakes its way through the wooden houses. After less than 150m you will emerge at the main road (Soi Wat Kalayanimit) where you must turn right to the temple of the same name. If you lose your way just ask any of the locals for Wat Kalayanimit.

5 WAT KALAYANIMIT

The majestic old riverside temple of Wat Kalayanimit actually predates Bangkok, although it was subsequently renovated in the 19th century, during the reign of Rama III, to house an enormous seated statue called Luang Paw Toh or Big Buddha. The Chinese also worship the statue and hold a grand homage-paying fair annually in its honour. Inside are fine murals and several Chinese shrines. Outside, in the spacious compound, the large bronze bell is reputed to be the largest in Thailand.

Walk to the river bank, less than 100m away, from where you will see some house barges.

6 HOUSE BARGES

Once to be found all along the waters of the Chao Phraya river, old rice barges are now the exception rather than the rule. The few that remain still ply the 'Mother of Rivers' carrying sand, charcoal and rice all the way down from Nakhon Sawan in the Central Plains.

From the house barges, walk east (downriver) along a narrow path that runs to the Tahrua Kalaya landing. Catch the regular baht boat that crosses back over the Chao Phraya river to Tha Rachini pier and the Pak Khlong Market. Having perused the stalls, catch a taxi or tuk tuk home.

Bangkok Bars by Night

This takes you to Patpong, the best-known nightspot in the city. Countless bars, restaurants and market stalls are to be found on all sides.
Allow 3 hours.

Catch a taxi or tuk tuk *to the intersection of Silom Road and Patpong 1 Road from where you can explore one of the world's best-known red light districts.*

1 PATPONG ROAD
Patpong is made up of three streets owned by an old Chinese rice-milling family known as the Pongs. Family patriarch Pong Pat bought the land as rice fields in the 1940s when Silom, the major road artery, was still a canal. Today the area has become the largest, most successful and most popular tourist destination in Thailand – and the Pong family one of the richest in Asia.
To get a sense of the place wander down Patpong Road, ignoring all the touts, then stop at the Limelight Bar, which is situated on the ground floor about 50m up on the left.

2 LIMELIGHT BAR
This is one of the oldest bars in the district, but with the modern décor that has become a hallmark of the changing times. When the first strip bar opened in 1969, the police tried to ban it. These days 'go-go dancing' is the rule in Patpong rather than the exception. Try a Mekong whisky and coke, but as with every other bar in Patpong check the price first.
Leave Limelight, cross the road and turn left where you will find King's Castle 50m further down on the ground floor.

3 KING'S CASTLE
Although *Newsweek* voted this the best bar in town several years ago, King's Castle is better known as the spot where Carol Thatcher, the daughter of the former British prime minister, was allegedly involved in a 'balloon show'. That was back in 1984 and the balloon show has since moved to other upstairs bars. Meanwhile, King's Castle continues to thrive.
Leave King's Castle, turn right and recross the road.

Approximately 50m further on you will find Mizus.

4 MIZUS

History places the beginning of Patpong at the door of Mizus. It was set up in 1954 and has continued selling western food and Japanese specialities ever since. Do not expect girls though. Mizus is strictly for eating and taking in the past in a cosy atmosphere. Try a steak or one of the Japanese house specialities.
Leave Mizus and turn left to the Blue Sky Thai Boxing Bar.

5 BLUE SKY THAI BOXING BAR

Thai boxing may be alien to Patpong, but then anything goes here. Get there before 10pm, when the show generally begins, and get a seat by the ring. *Muay-Thai* here may not be as skillful as in Bangkok's better known Lumphini and Ratchadamnoen stadiums, but for those with limited time it provides an idea of the skills involved. Between boxing bouts there are generally other forms of entertainment.
When you have seen enough boxing, explore the shopping stores that line the street.

Traditional martial arts survive in the form of Thai boxing, *muay-Thai*

6 MARKETS

Patpong is especially famous for its fake watches, T-shirts and cassettes. Understandably, it is pointless to expect the same quality as the originals. Remember always to bargain and smile as much as you can (you generally get better bargains that way).
Once you have had your surfeit of markets, round the evening off at the Queen's Castle, which sits close by Limelight near the corner of Patpong and Silom Road on the first floor.

7 QUEEN'S CASTLE

Queen's Castle is renowned for its live shows and for all the things people generally expect to find in Patpong. Normally it is packed with foreigners and is reasonably priced, but as with every bar check prices on entry. In the old days many of the first floor rooms in Patpong were taken up by journalists' offices. These days few of them would be able to afford the high rent.
Leave the Queen's Castle and either take a taxi home or explore some of the other establishments. Beware touts who take you to second-floor 'clip joints' and try to charge you the earth. Always check prices for drink and entertainment first and if in doubt do not go in.

From Bangkok to the River Khwae

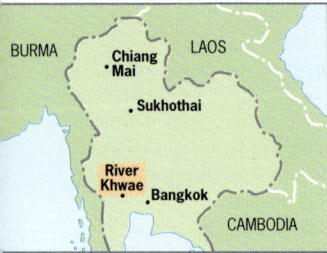

This takes you by train to the historic bridge over the River Khwae (Kwai), for a short trip down the river and a visit to the war cemetery, and return to Bangkok. *Day trip.*

Catch a taxi or express boat to Thonburi Train Station (also known as Bangkok Noi) on the western side of the Chao Phraya river and buy a day return ticket to Kanchana Buri.

Breakfast at the Thonburi Market, next door to the railway station, then catch the train that departs at 7.45am sharp for Kanchana Buri and Nam Tok. The carriages are third-class. No reservations are possible.

1 THE KANCHANA BURI EXPRESS

Leaving the old capital of Thonburi, the train cuts west into the area known as the central plains, going as far as Nam Tok, a small village marking the end of the line.

At Nakhon Pathom, which you reach after one hour, you will glimpse a vast pagoda on the left. This is one of the biggest in the world and was built on the spot where Buddhism was first brought to Thailand in the 3rd century BC by missionaries sent out by the Emperor Asoke of India.

The train continues through rice paddies and tapioca plantations, first stopping at Kanchana Buri then, three minutes later, at the Khwae Bridge Station where you should get out.

2 KHWAE BRIDGE

This, the most famous and chilling bridge in modern history, was built in 1943 by Allied prisoners of war for the Japanese. The central spans of the bridge were blown up in 1945 and subsequently rebuilt with war reparation funds. The

rest of the bridge is original and it continues to be used by trains and pedestrians. Note the old steam engine, at the outdoor museum alongside the station, which was used during World War II.
Walk over the Khwae Bridge and explore the other side. Then walk down the river to the restaurant and boat landing stage.

3 RIVER KHWAE
The tributaries Khwae Yai and Khwae Noi join at Kanchana Buri to form the Mae Klong river. For a pleasant hour's trip, hire a long-tailed boat from near the restaurant and ask to be taken on the standard trip to the cave, the cemetery and the museum.
As you go downriver the boat will take the right fork up the Khwae Noi until you reach Wat Thum Khao Phun on the right.

4 WAT THUM KHAO PHUN
The main attraction of this *wat* is a small and poorly lit cave. Years ago it was rumoured to contain gold left by the fleeing Japanese army at the end of World War II. Like many caves in Thailand it has Buddha images placed in many of the recesses.
From Wat Thum Khao Phun, the boat will take you to the Chung Kai Allied War Cemetery.

5 CHUNG KAI WAR CEMETERY
More than 16,000 prisoners of war lost their lives building the so-called 'Death Railway'. They are remembered in two graveyards built by the Commonwealth War Graves Commission and beautifully maintained. Some of the 1,750 memorial stones in the Chung Kai Cemetery bear the 'Known unto God' inscription used for unknown soldiers.
Leaving the war cemetery the boat will take you back to the junction of the two rivers and up the Mae Klong to the Jeath War Museum.

6 JEATH WAR MUSEUM
Established by the venerable Phra Thep Panyasuthee, in memory of the prisoners who lost their lives, the museum houses a collection of items related to the construction of the railway. The bamboo huts are replicas of those used by Allied prisoners of war. The paintings inside give some idea of their human suffering. Outside are weapons and an old field telephone.
Leaving the war museum the boat will take you back to the Khwae Bridge Railway Station, from where the train departs for Bangkok in mid-afternoon, arriving back at Thonburi Railway Station at about 6pm. From the station catch a taxi or boat home.

'Death Railway' at Kanchana Buri

TOUR

Chiang Mai's Thaphae Road

This tour takes you on a stroll through Chiang Mai's famous markets and temples and to the popular night bazaar on Chiang Khlan Road. *Allow 1½ hours.*

Begin at Thaphae Gate opposite Ratchadamneon Road and walk east towards the Ping river down Thaphae Road.

1 THAPHAE GATE
One of five gates that were constructed in the 13th century, under King Mengrai, to defend his capital, Thaphae was said to have been built by 90,000 men working 24-hour shifts. That did not stop the Burmese knocking down the walls, gates and ramparts when they invaded the city in the early 18th century. What is left is a rather gruesome imitation of the original, but if you climb up the steps you can look down over the moated heart of the old city.

Turn down Thaphae Road, walking away from the centre for around 200m until you reach Wat Maharam on your right.

2 WAT MAHARAM
Although not one of Chiang Mai's better known temples, Wat Maharam does have a certain charm. It also shows the

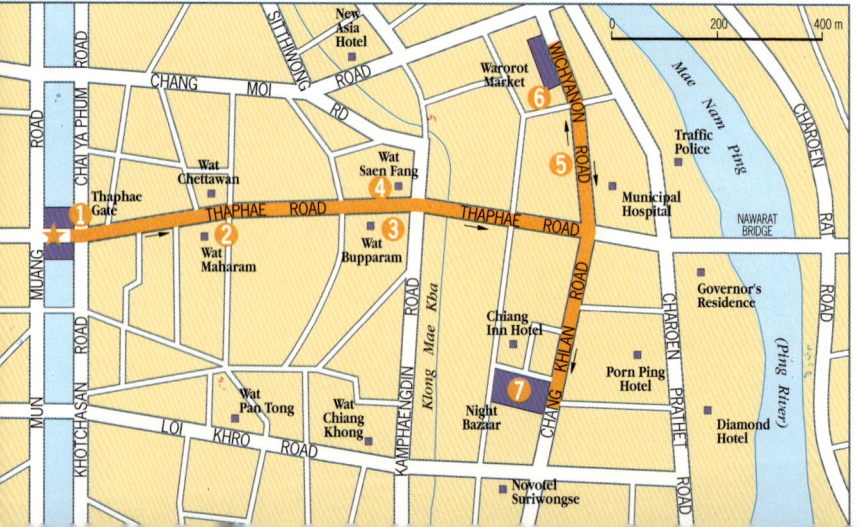

characteristic architectural shifts in style from the older Burmese *viharn* (temple hall) and *chedi* (pagoda) to the newer Lanna *bot* (main building). Running parallel to the *wat* is a quiet *soi* (alley) where you will hear the sound of birds and see a few old wooden houses.

Leave Wat Maharam and continue right down Thaphae Road for 300m. On the right you will see Wat Bupparam.

3 WAT BUPPARAM

Built during the 15th century, and renovated in the 18th century, Wat Bupparam is one of the finest examples of Lanna architecture, with its five-headed *naga* snakes, lanna-style roof and Burmese arches. Note the tiny old wooden *viharn* (temple hall) with its delicate engravings and, next door, a holy well whose waters are used for bathing the king.

Leave Wat Bupparam, turn right along Thaphae Road and walk 50m. Wat Saen Fang is on your left.

4 WAT SAEN FANG

An oasis of calm in the midst of busy Thaphae Road, Wat Saen Fang incorporates part of the second ring of city walls. Inside is a tall Burmese-style *chedi* (pagoda) and some cannons once used to defend the city. On the windows there are beautiful golden engravings, showing scenes from the *Ramayana* epic and from the *Jataka* tales, and on the door there are animals bringing water and honey to the meditating Buddha.

Leave Wat Saen Fang, turn left down Thaphae Road and continue for 300m past stalls selling amulets and wooden Buddha images. Turn left down Wichyanon Road.

5 WICHYANON ROAD

This is one of the most charming parts of the town, with its narrow alleys, old wooden houses and shops selling pirated cassettes of Western pop music as well as lottery tickets. This is a good place to buy silver bracelets and leather belts at low prices or to wander into the Chinese gold shops.

Walk along Wichyanon Road and bear left. After around 250m you will reach the covered Warorot Market.

6 WAROROT MARKET

The locals' treasure trove, Warorot is Chiang Mai's most authentic market, selling flowers, clothes, toys and, occasionally, delightful wooden bird cages. If you want to explore the fascinating side streets, just hire one of the tricycle taxis parked along the edge of the street.

Retrace your steps to Thaphae Road and cross over to continue down Chang Khlan Road for 300m. On the right you will see the Viang Ping Night Bazaar.

7 NIGHT BAZAAR

The three-floor emporium on Chiang Khlan Road is Chiang Mai's most popular shopping spot, stocking almost every sort of antique, cloth and trinket known to Thailand. Hilltribe artefacts are attractive buys and make ideal souvenirs. Look out for the little metal weights, in the shape of elephants and birds, on sale as opium measures. Many of the antiques here are smuggled over the border from Burma. Although most of the stalls are only active from 6pm onwards, there are always a few that are open all day to attract tourist custom. As usual, bargain vigorously for anything you fancy.

From the night bazaar, catch a tuk tuk *or* songthaew *(truck taxi) back to Thaphae Gate.*

Chiang Mai's Walled City by Tricycle

This takes you on a gentle tour around the heart of old Chiang Mai and to the temples that were once the centre of city life. *Allow 1½ hours.*

Hire one of the city's numerous tricycle taxis to take you on a circuit inside the city walls. The first stop is Wat Phra Singh, which lies at the intersection of Ratchadamnoen and Sing Harat Road.

1 WAT PHRA SINGH

Built in the 14th century, Wat Phra Singh is best known as the residence of the famous Buddha Phra Singh, a statue said to have been brought from Sri Lanka many centuries ago. Its head was stolen in 1922, but you can still see the replica. Inside the

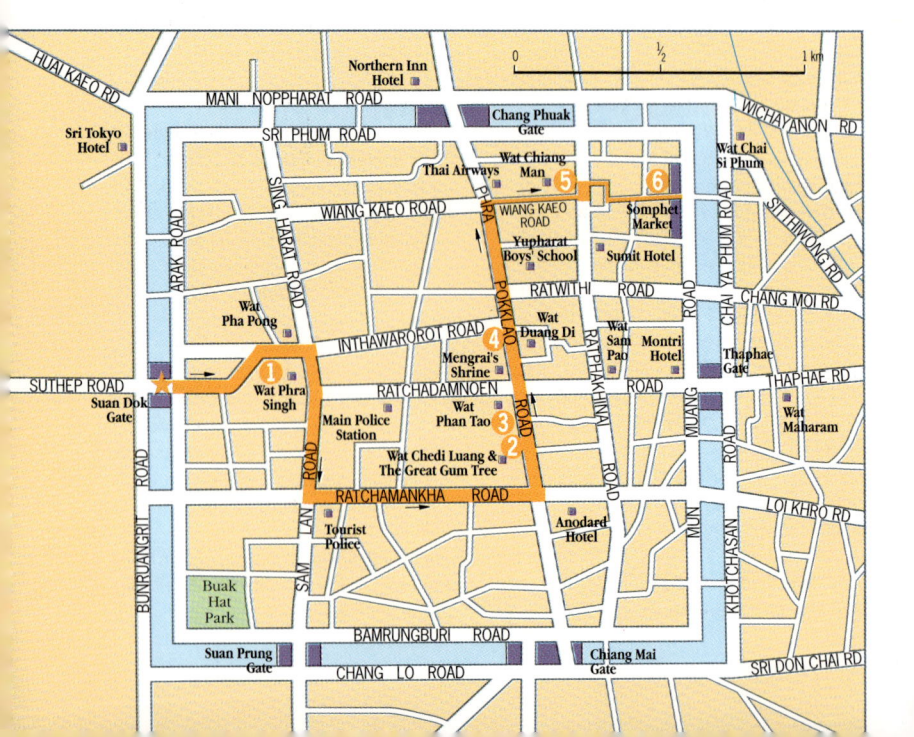

viharn (temple hall) is a collection of faded murals showing northern and Lanna customs, while outside is a charming 14th-century library.
Leaving the temple, turn right then first left down Ratchamankha Road. After 500m, turn left down Phra Pokklao Road where you will see Wat Chedi Luang.

2 WAT CHEDI LUANG

Until a great earthquake shook the very foundations of the temple in 1545, the massive *chedi* (pagoda) of Wat Chedi Luang dwarfed all others. It was built by King Saen Muang Mai (1385–1401) and at one stage contained the famous Emerald Buddha (now in Bangkok's Grand Palace). Inside the *bot* (main hall) you can make merit by putting gold leaf on the statue of Luangpoowaen, a well-known *bhikkhu* (monk).
Walk out of the temple into the gardens and you will see a vast gum tree tied with a ribbon around its trunk.

3 THE GREAT GUM TREE

This is the most famous and valued piece of wood in all Chiang Mai. Legend tells that so long as the tree stands, the town of Chiang Mai will thrive. Under the gum tree is the city pillar housed in a small building. It is customary to make a *wai* (greeting) or leave an offering of a wooden elephant or jasmine bouquet for the resident spirits.
Leave the temple compound and turn left. Continue for 50m past Wat Phan Tao, a small wooden temple with beautiful stuccoed and gilded decorations. A short distance further on you will reach a crossroads and Mengrai's Shrine.

4 MENGRAI'S SHRINE

The small gilded shrine that nestles on the intersection of Ratchadamnoen and Phra Pokklao Road recalls the great man who founded the city of Chiang Mai in 1296. Mengrai, according to popular legend, had it built in less than three years before going on to expand the kingdom of Lanna. Too great a man to suffer a normal fate, he was reputedly killed by lightning in 1311. Offerings of joss sticks are left in his memory.
From Mengrai's Shrine continue straight for 800m past Yupharat Boys' School (which occupies the site of the former palace) and turn right down Wiang Kaeo Road, also known as Phra Pokklao Lane. About 200m further down, you will see Wat Chiang Man on the left.

5 WAT CHIANG MAN

Reputedly the oldest *wat* in town, Wat Chiang Man is also one of the most delightful, with its quiet atmosphere and fragrant teakwood monks' quarters. The temple is especially famous for the Phra Setang Khamani (Crystal Buddha), a statue said to have the power to bring rain. Equally potent is said to be the Phra Sila (Marble Buddha), a figure that came from India about 1,000 years ago.
Leave Wat Chiang Man, turn left and cross over Ratphakhinai Road. Somphet Market is at the bottom on Mun Muang Road.

6 SOMPHET MARKET (TALAHT SOMPHET)

One of Chiang Mai's lesser-known markets, this has delicious food stalls and colourful flowers. Try a *somtam* made with grated mango, lemon and garlic: add a little chilli and feel the temperature rise. Afterwards wander down the little alleys that sell exotic fruits, grilled fish and kebabs.
From Somphet Market, catch a tuk tuk or songthaew (truck taxi) home or explore some of the surrounding area.

Circuit of Phuket

This tour, by jeep or trail bike, takes you from the historic old town to some of the wildest and most unspoilt beaches on Phuket. *Day trip.*

Start in Phuket Town on Ranong Road, park along one of the sideroads and briefly explore the town on foot.

1 PHUKET TOWN

Although it has undergone rapid development, Phuket Town has several beautiful old buildings, a witness to the days when it was a trading hub for the region. Try wandering down Ranong Road where the office of Thai Airways is an example of the Sino–Portuguese architecture that was fashionable during the late 19th century. Afterwards visit the market on Ranong Road and the Chinese temple of San Jao Jui Tui, scene of the famous annual vegetarian festival.
From Phuket town take route 402, signposted towards the airport. After 13km you will reach the roundabout on which stands the Heroines' Monument.

2 HEROINES' MONUMENT

If it were not for two sisters, Phuket might not be part of Thailand at all. In 1785, Jan and Muk withstood a month-long siege by the Burmese before they went on the attack, dressing up as men and routing the opposition. The grateful islanders have since erected this monument and they make offerings of wooden elephants to the duo.
From the Heroines' Monument continue along route 402 for 6km to Thalang.

3 THALANG

The one-time capital of Phuket, Thalang was besieged, pillaged and destroyed by Burmese invaders in 1899. Little is left of the original town but there are some charming old wooden houses and a strange Sino-Buddhist temple with

prangs (spires), dragons and golden bells.
From Thalang continue on route 402 for 1km until you see a small turning on the right, signposted to Wat Phra Thong.

4 WAT PHRA THONG

Phuket's Temple of the Gold Buddha is home to a famous half-buried Buddha image which was discovered when a young boy tethered his waterbuffalo to its top knot, only to die shortly afterwards. When the Burmese invaded in 1785 they attempted to steal the image, but were attacked by a swarm of angry hornets and driven off. Others who have tried to excavate the statue have met with similarly unfortunate consequences.
From Wat Phra Thong continue along route 402 for 5km, then turn left down route 4031. After 6km turn left down a steep road for Nai Thon.

5 NAI THON

Here you will find vestiges of old Phuket, with its beautiful coastline, inland rice paddies and water buffaloes, still relatively unscathed by the nearby building spree. Along the coast is a long sandy beach fringed by casuarina trees.
From Nai Thon continue along the road past secluded Bang Tao Beach. The road is steep and subject to erosion, but offers spectacular views. At Choeng Thale branch right and follow the signposts for 9km to Surin Beach.

6 SURIN BEACH

This is one of the more peaceful stretches of the island, surrounded by pretty coves but haunted by dangerous currents. The area borders a Thai Muslim village with a flavour quite different from the rest of the island. Wander down the shore and have a snack at one of the beach stalls selling delicious *somtam* (mango and garlic) and fish-head curry.
From Surin Beach continue along the coastal strip, past a beautiful little rock-dominated beach, and from there to Ban Kamala with its lovely stretch of sand. The road climbs steeply before descending at Patong Beach.

7 PATONG BEACH

The most garish and extreme face of Phuket, the 4km long crescent of Patong gained early popularity among sailors as a dry-season port. Now it attracts not only the US Navy but every other lover of watersports and entertainment, with its jetskiing, big hotels and nightlife.
From Patong take route 4029, then turn on to route 4020 which will take you back to Phuket town. Alternatively take the longer, more scenic route via Karon/Kata, Prom Thep Cape, Rawai and Chalong. If it is late, beware heavy traffic.

Two sisters led an 18th-century battle which preserved Phuket's independence

Cycling Around Sukhothai

This tour takes you around some of the most spectacular and least-visited ruins at Sukhothai, the first great kingdom of the Thais. *Allow 4 hours.*

Start at the market outside the historical park, hire a bicycle from one of the shops on the main road and head to Ramkamhaeng National Museum, signposted to the left just off the roundabout.

1 RAMKAMHAENG NATIONAL MUSEUM

Built in 1960 in memory of Sukhothai's greatest king, the Ramkamhaeng National Museum contains a superb collection of Sukhothai sculpture brought from Sukhothai, Si Satchanalai and Kamphong Phet. Note the magnificent 14th-century 'walking' Buddha just inside the entrance, the famous inscription and the stucco decorations which have become the hallmark of Thailand's most graceful period of art (see page 92).
Leave the museum and, at the roundabout, turn left into the historical park. Wat Mahathat is 250m further on to the left.

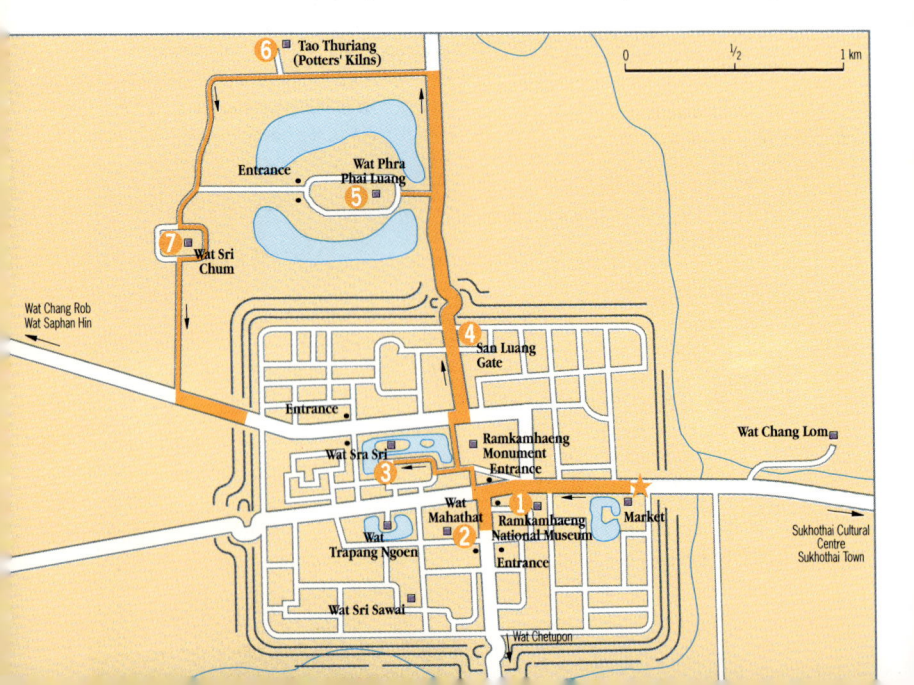

2 WAT MAHATHAT AND THE ROYAL PALACE

This is the largest, and for many the most beautiful, of Sukhothai's temples. Built in the 13th century by Sri Indrathit, 'Father of Dignitaries', it sits among lotus-filled ponds, has 198 *chedis* (pagodas) and was formerly the home of a vast, seated bronze Buddha.

From Wat Mahathat return to the intersection and take the minor road almost directly opposite. Take the first left and 350m further on, you will see Wat Sra Sri.

3 WAT SRA SRI

Situated on two connected islands, Wat Sra Sri (Temple of the Splendid Pond) contains a monumental seated Buddha gazing peacefully out past rows of columns to the water beyond.

From Wat Sra Sri retrace your steps and turn left at the signpost for San Luang Gate, which lies 600m further on.

4 SAN LUANG GATE

The northern gate and entry to the city, San Luang (House of the Royal Spirit) forms part of the extensive earthen ramparts which originally surrounded Sukhothai.

Continue along the road past the San Luang Gate and you will come to Wat Phra Phai Luang situated 500m further on to the left.

5 WAT PHRA PHAI LUANG

Known as the Temple of the Great Wind, this is one of the city's oldest monasteries and was originally built by the Khmers as a Hindu temple. Among the ruins spread over a vast area of grass you can can still see the ramparts, surrounded by a moat, typical of the religous architecture of the time. Note the northern *prang* (spire) decorated with stucco Hindu and Buddhist figures.

Leave the wat and cycle around the moat. After 100m turn left. 500m further on you will see the kilns at Tao Thuriang.

6 POTTERS' KILNS

Excavations have so far brought to light 49 kilns, spread over an area of 3 hectares. These were first used before AD1300 and produced a special kind of *celadon* (green-glazed ware) with pots distinguished by the imprint of a fish or flower on the base.

Leave Tao Thuriang and continue for 1.3km to Wat Sri Chum, situated on the right.

7 WAT SRI CHUM

This *wat* is famed for its awesome Buddha housed within a massive square *mondop* (shrine). The image, known as Phra Achana or Venerable Buddha, measures 11.3m from knee to knee, is 15m tall and is rumoured to have once halted a Burmese invasion. Inside the walls of the shrine, which are 3m thick, is a secret passage whose ceiling is engraved with scenes from the *Jataka* tales.

Leave Wat Sri Chum and continue along the road. At the next intersection turn left back to the historical park. Hand back your cycles and catch a songthaew *home.*

Beautiful Wat Mahathat in Sukhothai

What to See Bangkok

*W*ith its golden temples, its endless traffic jams and its colourful canals, it is like no other city in Asia. It has around eight million inhabitants, over 400 temples and more than three million vehicles. You will either love or hate it, but you should never miss it.

King Rama I established his capital on the banks of the Chao Phraya river in 1782, shortly after the fall of Ayutthaya. At the time it was little more than a fishing village, but the king built palaces and canals, parks for his elephants and statues of Buddha.

Successive monarchs added further royal residences, tree-lined malls and great temples, pushing the resident Chinese further out of the centre and extending the city on both sides of the Chao Phraya. The Victorians knew it as the 'Venice of the East'.

Much has changed in the intervening period. Since the 1970s, especially, the city has undergone a massive economic boom; canals have been filled in to make way for roads and highrises built to accommodate the massive influx of people from the provinces. Yet the temples remain, along with many of the waterways and all the charms and excesses of one of Southeast Asia's last great oriental cities.

The best sights

Bangkok is not an easy place to explore, but it is one where effort is correspondingly rewarded. If time is short the Grand Palace, the canals at Thonburi and the temple of Wat Arun should not be missed. These are to Bangkok what the Eiffel Tower is to Paris and the Houses of Parliament to London.

Other temples, crowded markets, and statues made of huge quantities of gold are strewn around the city, rewarding those with greater time to explore.

One experience, however, that no visitor should miss is a morning's shopping, for Bangkok is one of the most exotic and cheapest purchasing centres in the East. Another is the opportunity to try some of the best and spiciest Thai food. Evening is the time to visit the

The spires of the Royal Palace, across the Chao Phraya from Wat Arun

WHAT TO SEE

Bangkok as seen from the top of Wat Saket

bars, the discos or masseuses for which the metropolis is justifiably renowned.

Many visitors find the easiest way to get around the city is by organised tour. That way at least you will be spared the problem of negotiating the labyrinthine side streets and crowded buses. Tours will show you all the best-known landmarks, without the heat and exhaust fumes. Most tours include lunch at a Thai restaurant and will almost always drop you off at your hotel.

Ultimately, however, the real Bangkok is something felt, not seen, something best explored by yourself with time on your hands and with endless reserves of patience.

A special energy

Bangkok has a special energy about it, a frenzied chaos that you will find in few other places around the world, but there can be also a genuine calm about it. Vast traffic jams line the streets off Silom Road while, near by, girls sell orchids by the river.

Then there are the special smells, the whafting of kebabs, the car fumes, the markets, the smiles; whimsical, loud, calm. One minute you can be breathing in the exhaust of a thousand revving vehicles and the next emerge in the calm of Lumphini Park or surrounded by the old-worldly grandeur of Jim Thompson's House.

Indeed the city is only playing out the true meaning of its name (the longest recorded in the *Guinness Book of Records*). Rama I called his capital 'Great city of angels, the supreme repository of divine jewels, the great land unconquerable, the grand and prominent realm, the royal and delightful capital city full of nine noble gems, the highest royal dwelling and grand palace, the divine shelter and dwelling of the reincarnated spirits.'

Wherever you go and whatever you do, Bangkok will build on that description. It is an assault on the senses and the expectations, a battering of the old and the new and, more than anything, it is a reflection of the Thais themselves: colourful, vibrant and, at the last count, enigmatic.

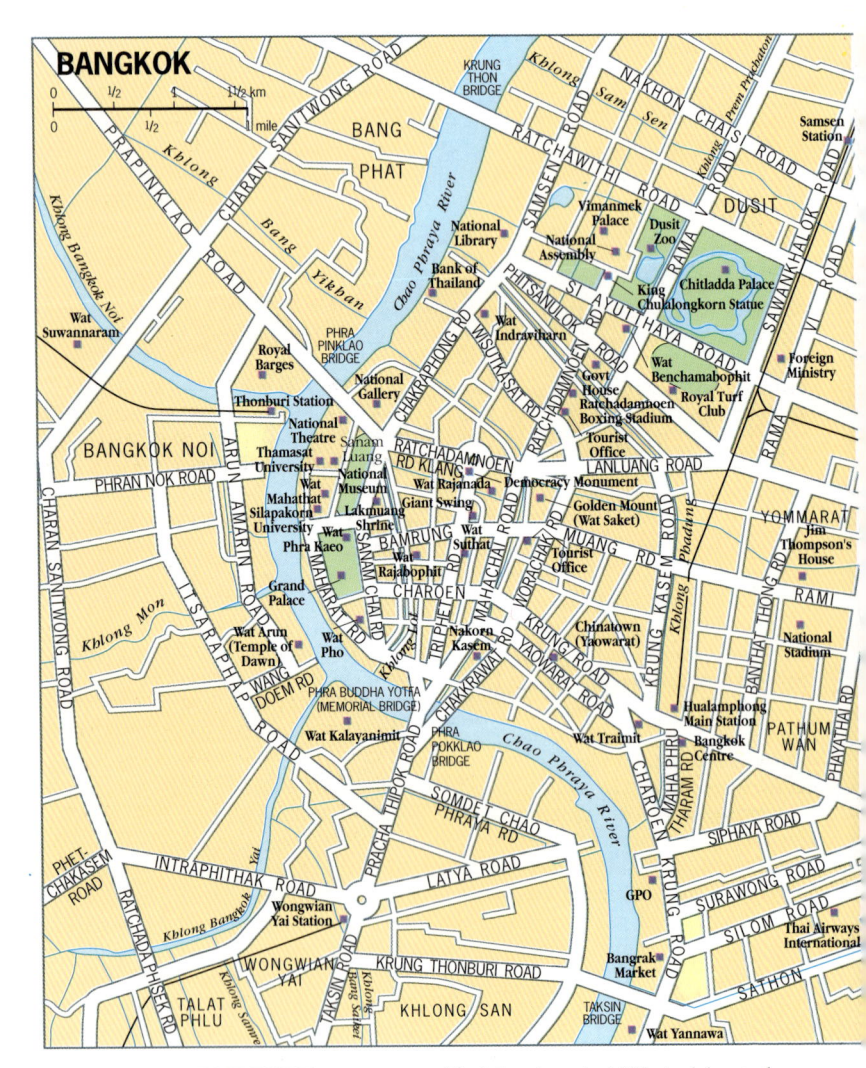

CELESTIAL RESIDENCE
(Vimanmek Mansion)

One of the most delightful sights in the city, Vimanmek is more the sort of thing you expect to find in a European capital than an oriental city. Built by King Chulalongkorn in 1901, it claims to be the world's largest teakwood building and stands by a lake in spacious grounds. Chulalongkorn lived here for only a few years but, under the patronage of Queen Sirikit, the building has been restored to

WHAT TO SEE

LEAD AND LUXURY

It starts at 6.30am: wave after wave of vehicles, motorbikes and *tuk tuks* streaming into the city. Lead pollutes the sky, pollutes the roads and gets into the very soul of the place known as Krungthep, the 'City of Angels'.

Probably no other city in the world can compare. Bangkok has more traffic, worse pollution, more people and it is growing faster than ever in its history.

In some parts of town, near the river, luxurious flats go for sky-high monthly rents. In others, shadowed under the condominiums, whole families struggle to live on a pittance.

Every year the number of migrant workers increases along with the lead and the luxury. By the end of the century, Bangkok is likely to have a population of 13 million.

Many of the migrant workers scrape a living selling drinks or plates of noodles, tranforming great areas of the city into small villages where they keep chickens and run food stalls. Others work as labourers on building sites. But even for them Bangkok remains the city of hopes and the city where dreams can come true.

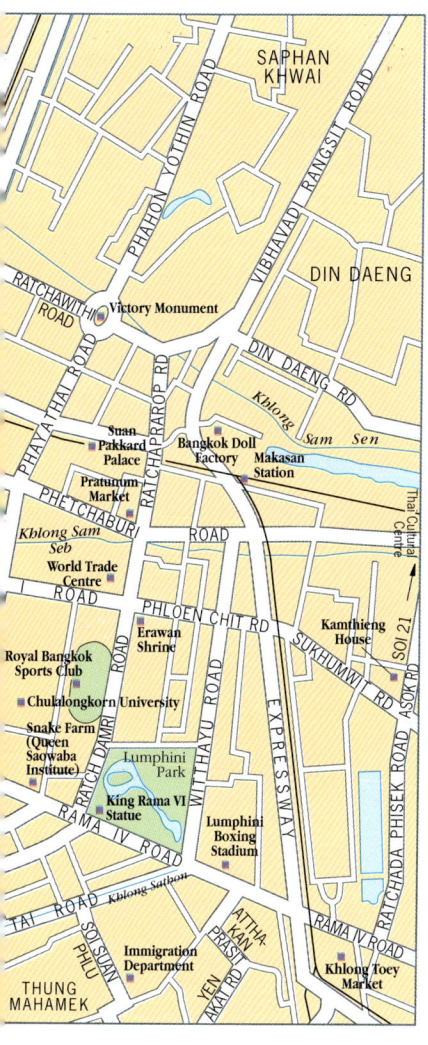

its former glory. Inside is an impressive collection of paintings, *objets d'art* and royal jewellery, as well as the royal bathroom equipped with a shower – believed to be the first ever installed in Thailand. The tank was manually filled to provide sufficient water for the royal dowse. Vimanmek is surrounded by water on all sides including the Channel of Fragrant Wood Canal, the Sheet of Glass Canal, the Channel of Silver, and – best known of all – the Jade Basin, named after the water's greenness.
Location: diagonally opposite the Dusit Zoo, behind the handsome old National Assembly building. Open: daily, 9.30am–3.15pm. Admission charge (Grand Palace ticket allows entry).

CHINA TOWN

Originally the Chinese lived up near the Grand Palace, but they were moved by Rama I to make way for the royal residences. The Chinese continue, however, to occupy the most colourful and frenetic part of the city, made up of a labyrinth of narrow streets, wooden houses and crowded lanes. Here you will find small shrines, a gold exchange and a profusion of markets selling strange healing remedies for acne and infertility as well as powdered wigs and sharks' fin soup. Bring a camera and be prepared for crowds.

For a glimpse of the most colourful quarters, wander down one of the side streets off Yaowarat Road. It is so busy you will not want transport.
Location: between Charoen Krung (New Road) and Yaowarat Road (see also pages 24–5).

A food shop in China Town

DISORIENTATION

Roads in Bangkok are not always what they seem. Some have three names, others just a number. The situation reflects the lack of city planning. There are, however, several points to remember. Turnings off the main roads are almost invariably called *sois* (lanes or alleys). Each has a number and all the odd-numbered *sois* are located on one side of the road, the even-numbered sois on the other. Almost all addresses include both the house number and the soi number. One without the other is unusable. To make certain where you are going, check on a map, bring a telephone number along and, if possible, get instructions written in Thai. Most hotels will be able to help you.

DUSIT ZOO

The Dusit Zoo contains the capital's biggest collection of wildlife. Inmates include elephants, rhinos and gibbons as well as a variety of exotic birdlife, plants, a komodo dragon and several dozen crocodiles. Children especially will be thrilled by the snack stores and the paddle boats. Visit the zoo on a weekend to see crowds of locals throwing peanuts to the crocodiles, holding hands and teasing the monkeys.

Near by are the Dusit Palace and the Chitladda Palace, the present residence of the royal family (closed to the public).
Location: Rama V Road. Open: daily, 8am–6pm. Admission charge.

ERAWAN SHRINE

Shrines in Bangkok are as numerous as houses, but the Erawan Shrine is nothing short of the city's most popular spirit

WHAT TO SEE

house. It was constructed after a stream of mishaps struck the nearby Erawan Hotel including the sinking of a boat carrying marble from India. Since proving its effectiveness (there have been no further untoward incidents), the Erawan Shrine has since become a popular spot with supplicants from around the city who come to donate wooden elephants (and occasionally even boiled eggs). The really devout hire dancers to make merit on their behalf.
Location: just ask for the Grand Hyatt Erawan Hotel on Ratchadamri Road, which is next door. Open: daily, 7am–11pm. Admission free.

GIANT SWING

Facing the giant *bot* (chapel) of Wat Suthat is the incongruous red swing known as the Sao Ching Cha or Giant Swing. This was originally used for a Brahmin ceremony held once a year in which Shiva and Vishnu were supposed to visit the temple. Teams would swing higher and higher in their effort to clutch a bag of money with their teeth. Since several participants were seriously injured when they fell off, the spectacle was abolished.

A devotee at the Erawan Shrine

Location: off a square at the end of Bamrung Muang Road. Open: daily, 9am–5pm. Admission free.

A moment of tranquillity in Dusit Zoo

Grand Palace

The most dazzling of all Bangkok's monuments, the Grand Palace lies behind massive white battlements in the heart of the old city. Built by successive monarchs of the Chakri dynasty, each crowning the glories of the last, it contains palaces and temples whose architecture spans over 200 years. It also contains the most precious single image in the whole of Thailand, the Emerald Buddha.

Indeed until King Rama IX, the present king, moved his residence to Chitladda Palace, following the unexplained death of his elder brother, Ananda Mahidol, it also housed the early monarchs.

Even today, the Grand Palace remains the true centre of royalty, used for state banquets and for the presentation of ambassadorial credentials. All the most important celebrations are held here and even the simplest occasion, such as the king's birthday, recalls all the pageantry of ancient Siam.

A succession of palaces

Several great monuments dominate the palace grounds, each with its own architectural style, reflecting both the times and the tastes of its founder.

The fabled spires of the Grand Palace

One of the finest is the Chakri Maha Prasad, built during the reign of King Chulalongkorn (1868–1910). This was designed by a British architect, but in Italian Renaissance style, reflecting the king's love of European architecture. On to this has been superimposed the Siamese-style *prasad* (tower). Inside are reception rooms and the throne room where the king still receives foreign ambassadors on a niello throne under a nine-tiered white umbrella.

To the right of Chakri Maha Prasad is the Dusit Maha Prasad, a classical Thai palace, built in 1789; alongside is an exquisite pavilion called the Arporn Phimok Prasad or 'Disrobing Pavilion', used by the king to remove his ceremonial hat.

Another fine building, and the only one currently open to visitors, is the Audience Hall of Amarin, built during the reign of Rama I (1782–1809). Everything about it speaks of regal splendour. Formerly the royal Court of Justice, it is now used as the coronation room or for royal ceremonies (at which the king once presided from a throne concealed by curtains).

Beyond the Audience Hall lies the inner compound, the mysterious quarters in which female members of the royal families, royal concubines and court women once resided. Until the beginning of this century, men were absolutely forbidden to enter the area. Times have changed and these days, although still closed to the general public, it is used by students of the Phra Tamnak Suankularb School who specialise in the ancient court arts.

The Emerald Buddha

The *pièce de résistance*, and the most precious of all images in Thailand, is housed in the northeast corner of the palace compound, within Wat Phra Kaeo.

The Emerald Buddha was supposedly discovered centuries ago in northern Thailand when a bolt of lightning struck an old *chedi* (pagoda) revealing the image. The Buddha was briefly housed in the northern cities of Chiang Rai, Lampang and Chiang Mai, before being taken to Luang Prabang and Vientiane by the Laotians. Finally it was recovered and installed, amid great pomp, by Rama I in Bangkok.

Do not expect some vast emerald statue though. The Buddha is actually made of green jade, measures just 0.75m tall and is contained high up on a gilded altar beneath an umbrella of gold.

Invested in this fragile figure is a supernatural power beyond all others: it is believed that, so long as the Emerald Buddha remains in Thai hands, the kingdom will be free.

It is hardly surprising, then, that the image is surrounded in splendour. On

Dazzling and glittering Wat Phra Kaeo

the walls are paintings from the great *Ramakien* epic while outside there are gold-embellished engravings and statues of mythological *kinarees* – half-bird, half-woman – said to inhabit the legendary Himalayan forests.

Photography is not allowed within Wat Phra Kaeo, but outside there is always a queue of people trying, surreptitiously, to aim their lenses between the gold panelled doors.
Location: five minutes walk from the Tha Chang express boat pier on the Chao Phraya river and within easy reach of Wat Pho, Wat Arun, Wat Mahathat, Lakmuang and the National Museum. Wear reasonably formal clothes (no shorts or sleeveless tops). Open: daily, 8.30–midday and 1–3.30pm. Admission charge.

Jim Thompson's is the place for Thai silk

JIM THOMPSON'S THAI HOUSE
One of the most famous residents of Bangkok in the mid-20th century was a man named Jim Thompson, a silk merchant, spy and connoisseur of fine antiques. He disappeared under mysterious circumstances in Malaysia's Cameron Highlands in 1967 but left behind him a beautiful old teak house.

The house is full of works of oriental art, pots and statues dating as far back as the Lop Buri period (11th–14th century). It overlooks a silk weaving 'village' in the heart of the city, where skeins of brightly coloured silk are hung out to dry. It has a small and luxuriant garden, and provides a wonderful feel of old Bangkok. Guided tours are offered in several languages.

Afterwards you may be guided to Jim Thompson's shop on Surawong Road to buy the silk for which he became known. Beware imitations and beware other shops that claim to be supplied by Jim Thompson's.
Location: Soi Kasem San 2, opposite the National Stadium on Rama I Road. Open: Monday to Saturday, 9am–5pm. Admission charge.

KAMTHIENG HOUSE
Kamthieng House is another of the city's great old teak residences dating back more than 200 years and representing one of the finest examples of northern Thai architecture.

The house was originally brought down from the northern provinces to illustrate the typical old Thai lifestyle with its sheds, its barn and its agricultural implements. Displays consist of old costumes and carvings along with the *ham yong* or 'sacred testicles' (carved lintels) said to preserve the fertility of its inhabitants.
Location: 141 Soi Askoke (Soi 21), Sukhumwit Road. Open: Tuesday to Saturday, 9am–noon and 1–5pm. Admission charge.

LAKMUANG SHRINE
When Rama I founded Bangkok, he placed the trunk of a laburnum tree in the ground to commemorate the event and to appease the resident spirits. Lakmuang (which literally means 'City Pillar') has since been enlarged, but remains the place from which all distances in Thailand are measured and it is hallowed above almost any other spot in Bangkok. Inside are several shrines where supplicants offer flowers, boiled eggs, joss sticks and, occasionally, bottles of whisky.

Location: at the southeast corner of the Pramane Grounds outside the Ministry of Defence on Sanam Luang. Open: daily. Admission free.

LUMPHINI PARK

A haven of calm in the centre of chaos, Lumphini Park is the principal area of greenery in the city. It lies within a stone's throw of the commercial centre, yet has a lake for boating, noodle stalls and shady walkways. Popular in the evening for running and in the afternoon for picnics, the park is at its most crowded at dawn when people come to practice *tai chi* (shadow boxing) and drink snakes blood from the stalls outside. For those with less athletic tastes, Soi Sarasin, the road that runs parallel to the northern exit also hosts some of the best jazz bars in town.
Location: on the corner of Silom Road and Rama IV opposite the Dusit Thani Hotel. Open: daily. Admission free.

MARKETS

The biggest and best-known market in Bangkok is the Weekend Market at Chatuchak Park off Phahon Yothin Road, active from 6am to dusk on Saturdays and Sundays. This is the place to pick up old books as well as plants, acne cures, parrots and anything else that you could possibly dream of.

For clothes, try Pratunam Market at the intersection of Ratchaprarop and Phetchaburi Road and for flowers and vegetables the Pak Khlong market at the foot of Memorial Bridge. For antiques, the Thieves Market off Yaowarat Road in China Town is still the favourite. Alternatively just wander off any of the main streets. At some stage you are bound to bump into a small neighbourhood market.

Relax, unwind and forget the traffic of Bangkok, in Lumphini Park

National Museum

A five-minute walk from the Grand Palace will bring you to one of the largest and finest museums in Southeast Asia. The National Museum houses a vast collection of exhibits and its English explanations offer the best starting point for anyone who wants to understand something of Thailand's cultural and artistic history.

In all, the exhibits cover more than 10,000 years, from the earliest traces of neolithic man up to the present day and they represent the best of the nation's works of art. Other provincial museums in Chiang Mai, Sukhothai, Korat and Khon Kaen also have priceless exhibits, but they cannot compare in size or scope.

Indeed the chief problem is that there is almost too much to absorb. Enthusiasts go back several times and then they go back for more. But even a small dip into the collection will be rewarded with invaluable insights into Thai culture, as well as providing an inkling of the power, ingenuity and serenity behind the monuments you see today.

A work of art

The starting point for any tour could well begin with the museum itelf. The buildings were formerly part of an old palace belonging to the surrogate monarch (the king's deputy – a post later abolished) and dating from 1782. Finest among them is the Buddhaisawan Chapel, with murals depicting scenes from the life of Buddha. Visitors should also try to view the Tamnak Deang or 'Red House', a splendid wooden structure dating from the reign of Rama I (1782–1809).

The next stop should be the

The museum contains artefacts from the Neolithic Age to the present Chakri dynasty

fantastical skulls, the bronzes and the pottery excavated from Ban Kao and Ban Chiang, evidence of a civilisation which may have thrived as far back as 10,000 years ago. These are to be found near the entrance, in the prehistory section, along with details about early trading routes and kingdoms.

Elsewhere the museum is divided into the original buildings and the two new wings with a total of 42 different halls each reflecting a different theme or period of history.

In the new south wing you will see the stone and bronze images of the Khmers who occupied vast areas of the kingdom from the 8th to the 11th century. Rooms 7 and 8 of the north wing are devoted to the Sukhothai period and contain some of the most beautiful Buddha images ever sculpted.

Other things not to miss include the funeral chariots in Room 17 (the largest of which is 12m high, weighs 20.3 tonnes and took 290 people to move) and the warrior mounted on a life-sized elephant in Room 10. Outside that room there are shadow masks, a miniature train that King Mongkut (Rama IV) presented to Queen Victoria, old photographs, textiles, puppets and flags as well as royal games and musical instruments.

Taking a tour

If you get the chance, take an organised tour. This is by far the best and most informative way of exploring the museum.

Tours are conducted in English on Wednesday and Thursday; in French on Wednesday; German on Thursday; and Japanese on the first and second Wednesday of each month.

One of the museum's treasures, an ancient Buddha image

If you only have a couple of hours to spare it is essential to decide on your priorities. Those with more time (or who make repeat visits) will be duly rewarded.

Outside the museum is a snackbar serving reasonably priced Western and Thai food. Adjacent to the National Museum is the National Theatre where drama and performances of Thai classical dance are presented. Occasionally if you are lucky you may find that a display is scheduled. Ask at the Tourist Authority of Thailand (No 4 Ratchadamnoen Nok Avenue, tel: 282 1143) for details.

Location: on Na Phra That Road opposite the northwest corner of Sanam Luang, within easy walking distance of the Grand Palace, Lakmuang and Wat Mahathat. Open: Wednesday to Sunday, 9am–4pm.
Admission charge.

ROYAL BARGE NATIONAL MUSEUM

The magnificently adorned Royal Barges were once used for annual processions down the river. The King's barge, *Suphanahong* ('the Auspicious Swan') is one of the most important. It is about 44m long and 54 oarmen are used to row it. It is also the oldest and most ornately carved, with a great bauble dangling from the swan's beak at the front. The barges are now too frail for regular use, but still make a colourful spectacle on very special occasions, such as a royal birth.
Location: off Khlong Bangkok Noi on the Thonburi side of the Chao Phraya river. The best way there is by long-tailed boat from Tha Chang pier near the Grand Palace. Open: daily, 8.30am–4.30pm. Admission charge.

One of the spectacularly carved royal barges

SIAM SQUARE

With its cinemas, its fashionable boutiques and its shopping centres, Siam Square tops anywhere else in the city as the heart of the young, the new and trendy. This is the place to shop for up-market clothes, silks and handicrafts but McDonald's hamburgers, Pizza Huts and videos are also there in abundance. The square is especially busy at dusk and at weekends.

Silom Road – banks and traffic

SILOM ROAD

The heart of Bangkok's business district, known as Silom, is the place to find the big banks, airline offices and shopping centres. A part of Silom is also known as Bangrak, meaning district of love. It is possibly no coincidence that here lies Patpong, the best-known red light district in the world (see page 32). Even if it is not your scene, everyone has to visit it. You will not have seen Bangkok otherwise.

SNAKE FARM

Snakes can be found at the Thonburi Snake Farm or the Dusit Zoo, but the best of them are at the Queen Saowaba Institute. Visitors can watch the snakes being milked for serum on weekdays at 11am and 2.30pm or at 11am on public holidays and weekends. The snakes include massive cobras, vipers and even the deadly krait. They are not, however, just there for tourists. They also serve the vital purpose of supplying serum to medical centres around the kingdom.
Location: on the corner of Henri Durant Road and Rama IV Road. Open: daily, 8.30am–4pm. Admission charge.

SUAN PAKKARD PALACE

This collection of beautifully preserved wooden houses is incongruously

WHAT TO SEE

surrounded by cranes and new towerblocks. This was originally the home of the late Princess Chumphot of Nagara Svarga, an enthusiastic gardener as well as a collector of antiques.

The luxuriant grounds of the palace contain numerous rare plants from all over the world as well as the famous lacquer pavilion which was put together from portions of two decayed buildings. *Location: near the Phayatha intersection on Si Ayutthaya Road. Open: Monday to Saturday, 9am–4pm. Admission charge.*

SUKHUMWIT ROAD

Sukhumwit Road lies to the east of the Silom business district and covers a rambling shopping, entertainment and residential area. Big hotels, European restaurants and nightclubs are to be found in abundance, along with alternative night spots, such as the Soi Cowboy hostess bars (between Soi 21 and Soi 23) and the similar Nana Plaza complex (Soi 4).

At one end, Sukhumwit Road extends into Phloen Chit Road whilst to the east

A richly ornate lacquer pavilion in the grounds of Suan Pakkard

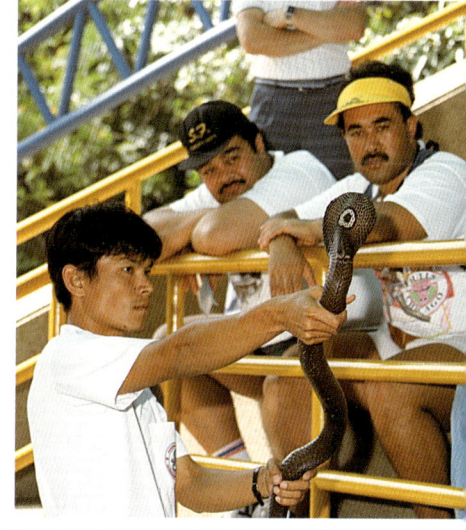

Tourists being shown a hooded cobra at the Snake Farm

it becomes a busy highway that runs all the way to the Cambodian border. All roads off Sukhumwit are numbered in *sois* (alleys) with the even numbers running to the south and the odd numbers to the north.

Temples

*B*angkok's six most renowned temples are scattered around the city. They can be seen as part of a tour (see page 26) or combined with other sights around the capital.

Wat Arun (Temple of Dawn)
Bangkok's best-known landmark and, until recently, its tallest building, Wat Arun is undoubtedly the most spectacular of the riverside temples.

Constructed during the 19th century and subsequently enlarged during the reigns of Rama II and III, its *prang* (spire) measures 79m, and is covered almost entirely with fragments of multicoloured porcelain. For good views of the river climb the steps, but be careful because they are very steep and slippery.
Location: directly opposite Tha Tien pier on the Thonburi side of the Chao Phraya river and is reached by baht boat. Open: daily, 8.30am–5pm. Admission charge.

A small, decorated temple beside Wat Arun

Wat Benchamabophit (Marble Temple)
One of the most recent of Bangkok's temples, Wat Benchamabophit was only started during the reign of King Chulalongkorn in 1901. It is built of milky white Carrara marble, shipped at great expense from Italy, which makes this *wat* one of the most beautiful and popular in the city.

Inside the courtyard are over 50 statues of Buddha and in the *bot* (main hall) are the ashes of King Chulalongkorn himself. The best time to visit is at dawn when the monks huddle under the trees on their early morning alms round.
Location: a short distance from the Dusit Zoo on Si Ayutthaya Road. Open: daily, 8am–5pm. Admission charge.

Wat Mahathat
Known as the Temple of the Great Relic, Wat Mahathat was built before Bangkok was founded and is renowned, above all, as a centre for Buddhist philosophy and meditation. Visit it on Sundays and Buddhist holidays when an open-air market is held outside the temple premises. Meditation classes are held in English on the second Saturday of the month, 2–6pm.
Location: on Na Pra That Road between the National Museum and Wat Phra Kaeo. Open: daily, 9pm–5pm. Admission free.

Wat Pho (Wat Chetupon)
The largest and one of the oldest of

WHAT IS A WAT

Thai temples have their own terms and meanings that can be as alien as the Thai language itself. A *chedi* or *stupa* is a bell-like tower or pagoda in which relics of the Buddha, or some other important person, are kept. A *prang* is a tall finger-like spire with a rounded top. A *chofa* is a graceful finial extending from the roof. A *prasad* is a tower sanctuary of Khmer origin. A *bot* is an ordination hall, and a *viharn* a hall for daily services.

Wat Arun contains many outstanding artistic treasures

Bangkok's temples, Wat Pho was founded by King Rama I in the 16th century and contains some of the capital's finest architecture.

The highlight is the gigantic Reclining Buddha that lies at the northern end of the enclosure. The figure measures more than 46m long and 15m high, and the soles of the feet have been inlaid with mother-of-pearl depicting the 108 auspicious signs of the Buddha.
Location: at the southern corner of the Grand Palace on Maharat Road. Open: daily, 8am–5pm. Admission charge.

Wat Saket

Perched on top of an artificial hill, Wat Saket, popularly known as the Temple of the Golden Mount, has fine views of the city and is an enclave of peace away from the hustle and exhaust fumes below. At the top is a gilded *chedi* (pagoda) enshrining sacred relics of the Buddha. The temple was started during the reign of Rama III, but was not completed until the reign of Rama V. To get there you must climb a flight of 318 steps.
Location: north of China Town on Ban Bart Road. Open: daily, 8am–5pm. Admission charge.

Wat Traimit

Wat Traimit's claim to fame is a 5.6-tonne Buddha made of gold and discovered in the 1950s when the East Asiatic Company took over the building. The image was originally encased in stucco but, while it was being moved by crane, it was dropped and the plaster casing broke revealing the massive solid gold image beneath.
Location: on the intersection of Yaowarat Road and Charoen Krung Road, near Hualamphong Railway Station. Open: daily, 9am–5pm. Admission free.

The spire of Wat Arun, encrusted with a glittering mosaic of broken glass and ceramic

BUDDHISM

In towns and cities all over Thailand, the first light of dawn brings lines of monks in their saffron robes on to the streets to begin their daily alms round. Men and women who have risen especially early to prepare foods, will place rice and fruit or flowers in the monk's bowl, bowing as they do so and asking for a blessing.

This pattern, repeated throughout the kingdom, has gone on for centuries.

Buddhism occupies a very special niche in Thai culture. It is more than just a religion – it can be a whole way of life or simply a way of hope.

Around 90 per cent of the population practice Theravada Buddhism in some way, either by giving robes to the monks or by giving them food. Acts of goodness, Buddhists believe, will be returned with deeds of good, and merits gained will bring more merit and the promise of a better life in the world to come.

In the *wats* (temples), men as young as 20 will join the order for anything from three weeks to a lifetime, meditating and strictly following the 227 Buddhist precepts in the quest for selflessness. Others, known as novices, will serve their time looking after the monks and receiving education.

Outside the order, Buddhism has few of the constraints that are part of other religions. But it is a part of everyday life and a way of showing, of feeling and of securing a better life.

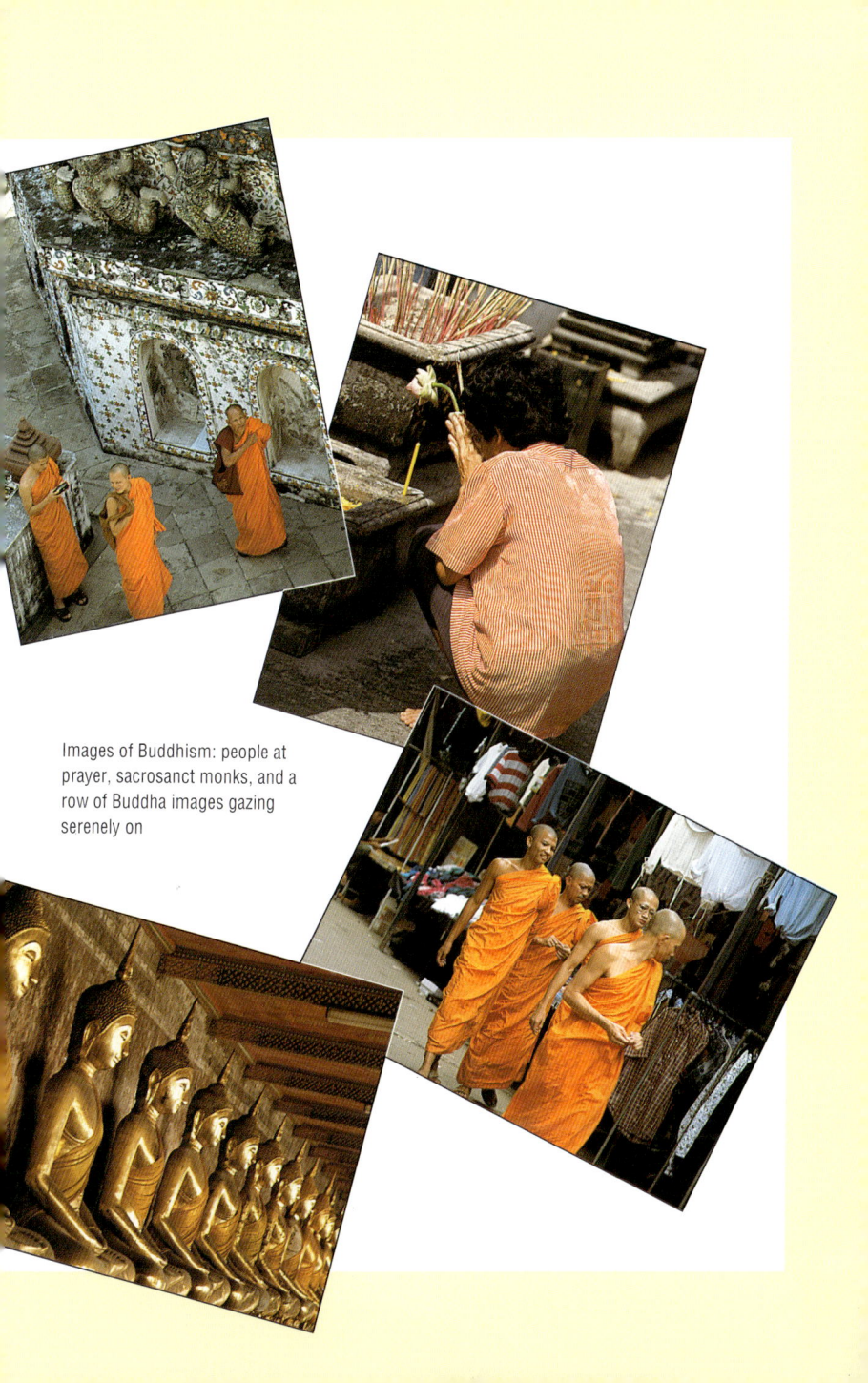

Images of Buddhism: people at prayer, sacrosanct monks, and a row of Buddha images gazing serenely on

Waterways

'The highways of Bangkok are not streets or roads, but rivers and canals' wrote Sir John Bowring in 1855. That may have been the case in the 19th century, but these days it is something of a simplification. Many of Bangkok's old *klongs* (canals) are now tarmac-covered highways, but a number of them have survived and travelling around them is still one of the great joys that the 'City of Angels' has to offer.

The main waterway is the Chao Phraya river which cuts through the city carrying rice barges down from the central plains. Off this main artery run the *klongs*, small waterways where life has changed little over the past decades.

Here you may see children swimming and older people cleaning themselves draped in sarongs. But if you are tempted to join them in the water think again. The Chao Phraya river is now so dirty that you would need a two week holiday just to recover.

On the *klongs*

The easiest way to get around the *klongs* is to catch one of the Chao Phraya express taxi boats that scurry up and down the river, stopping at the Oriental, the Sheraton and many other popular landmarks. These boats will take you all the way up to Nonthaburi and are very cheap (see page 28).

Travel on the river: the easiest way to get about in busy Bangkok

Alternatively, hire a long-tailed boat *(reua hang yao)* which will take you to the Thonburi floating market and the rural dwellings around Khlong Ban Dan and Khlong Bangkok Yai. Prices are higher and you pay by the hour.

Hotels also organise river trips to Ayutthaya as well as dinner cruises; advance booking essential.

Perhaps the most enjoyable way of exploring the waterways (and best value for money) is to take one of the public

long-tailed boats which, for a handful of *baht*, will take you to the smaller *klongs* where foreigners are the exception rather than the rule.

Public boats

The following public boats run regularly throughout the day and provide delightful glimpses of river life, although they may be crowded.

Chao Phraya River Express: departs from Wat Rajsingkron wharf every 15 minutes between 6am and 6pm stopping at 35 piers, including Tha Chang (Grand Palace) and Tha Thien (Wat Pho).

Klong Mon: departs every 30 minutes from Tha Thien Pier behind Wat Pho between 6.30am and 6pm. Sights include riverside temples and orchid farms.

Khlong Bang Koo Wiang and Khlong Bang Yai: departs Tha Chang pier near the Grand Palace every 30 minutes, between 6.15am and 10am. This trip passes the Royal Barge Museum.

Khlong Om: departs from Nonthaburi's Phibul Songkram pier every 15 minutes between 4am and 9pm. Attractions include durian plantations, temples and Thai-style houses.

Cross-river ferries: for short trips across the Chao Phraya river boats operate from Tha Thien pier to Wat Arun and from Tha Saphan Phut pier to Pracha Thipok Road.

Thonburi floating market

The pride of Bangkok's tourist industry became commercialised so many years ago that it has almost ceased to exist as a genuine market. Even so, the area around known as Khlong Bangkok Yai and Khlong Bangkok Noi (literally 'Big' and 'Little' canal) remains an endless

Thonburi's floating market, the early morning attraction which, after the temples, is probably Thailand's most celebrated spectacle

source of fascination with its coconut palms, old warehouses and new concrete Tudor-style residences studded haphazardly along the river bank. The floating market can be reached either by hiring a private long-tailed boat from along the river or by joining one of the group tours that leave at regular intervals from the Tha Chang pier outside the Grand Palace.

Tours and rented boats will take you to a snake farm and to the glorious Royal Barge Museum as well as stopping briefly at Wat Arun.

You will not be the only one doing the trip, but if you do not have the time to visit the more genuine market at Damnoen Saduak (see page 67) this is a wonderful way to get a glimpse of the old Bangkok, the Venice of the East.

BANGKOK ENVIRONS

AYUTTHAYA

Ayutthaya is not considered a highpoint in glorious Siam for nothing. The great city, once the nation's capital, survived 33 kings, numerous invasions and 400 years of turbulent history. In so doing, it established itself as one of major civilisations of the 14th to the 18th centuries.

Louis XIV of France sent his emissaries to the kingdom, while even the British and Portuguese traders came to buy spices and enjoy the largesse of its god-like rulers.

Only after numerous wars did the Burmese, invading on the backs of elephants, finally quell Ayutthaya in 1767. When they did so, they left little doubt as to who were the victors. All but 10,000 of the inhabitants were massacred or taken into slavery, gold Buddhas were melted down and the place was left in desolation.

Not everyone complains, though. Some people even think the city looks better in ruins than it might have done in its original state, with its weeds and dreams and its feel of days gone by.

Getting there

Ayutthaya is situated 76km north of Bangkok. Trains leave around 20 times a day from Hualamphong Railway Station and buses every 40 minutes from the Northern Bus Terminal on Phahon Yothin Road. The most popular way of getting there is by boat on the day trip run by the Oriental Hotel which leaves the hotel pier at 8am. Passengers return by coach around 6pm.
Reservations should be made at the Oriental Hotel, 48 Oriental Avenue (tel: 236 0400).

Getting around

If you are without your own transport, it is best to hire a tricyclist and ask for a short tour. These hardened peddlers know better than anyone what to see.

Chao Sam Phya Museum

This contains exquisite Ayutthaya-period stone and bronze Buddha images and a fine collection of carved door panels.
Location: on Rotchana Road. Open: Wednesday to Sunday, 9am–4pm. Admission charge.

Resplendent even in decay; the ruins of Wat Mahathat, Ayutthaya

The Summer Palace Pavilion, Bang Pa-in

Wat Mahathat
This temple was built by King Ramesuan in 1384. When the government undertook to restore the ruins in 1956, the *wat* was found to contain a buried chest containing a relic of lord Buddha inside a golden casket.
Location: on Naresuan Road. Open: daily, 8.30am–4pm. Admission charge.

Wat Ratburana
This was built in 1424 by King Borommaracha II to commemorate his two sons who killed each other in an elephant duel.
Location: opposite Wat Mahathat. Open: daily, 8.30am–4pm. Admission charge.

Wat Sri San Phet
The most important of Ayutthaya's temples, this once housed a vast gold standing Buddha, until the Burmese took a liking to it and melted it down. What remains are three *chedis* (pagodas) containing the ashes of King Borom Trai Lokanat and his two sons.
Location: off Sri San Phet Road. Open: daily, 8.30am–4.30pm. Admission charge.

Viharn Phra Mongkol Bophit
This is one of Thailand's largest bronze images; it was sacked in 1767 but has since been restored in its original style.
Location: off Sri San Phet Road. Open: daily, 8.30am–5pm.

Bang Pa-In Summer Palace
A short ride from Ayutthaya is the fabled summer palace of Bang Pa-In, the country residence of a succession of monarchs dating originally from the 17th century. The original palace was founded by King Prasat Thong.

The highlight is the exquisite 19th-century Aisawan Tippaya Asna pavilion. This sits in the centre of a lake, where King Chulalongkorn, a man known for his European tastes, would watch the world go by.

Near by is the classic-style royal residence of Warophat Phiman, the Saphakhan Ratchaprayun and the Ho Withun Thasana, endearingly known as the 'Sage's Lookout'.
Location: 20km to the south of Ayutthaya. Bang Pa-in is included in most tours. Minibuses also leave from the Chao Prom Market in Ayutthaya. Open: daily, 8.30am–3.30pm. Admission charge.

ANCIENT CITY

Billed as the largest outdoor museum in Thailand (and possibly in the world), Ancient City is a must for anyone with limited time, limited temple interest or a lot of children.

The city covers no less than 80 hectares and consists of scaled-down models of *wats*, palaces and ruins (as well as a few originals), laid out in an area the shape of Thailand. Even some buildings that no longer exist are on show, re-created from ancient records.

So heavily promoted is the Ancient City that many tourists go expecting to discover one of Thailand's ancient capitals. But if you are looking for an idea of the kingdom's vast architectural riches or a sense of the thousands of years of its history, you will undoubtedly find this one of the best sights in the vicinity.

Location: 34km to the southeast of Bangkok. Advice and information, as well as a guidebook to the Ancient City can be obtained from the Ancient City Co, Democracy Monument, Ratchadamnoen Avenue (tel: 226 1936). Alternatively catch bus number 8 or 11 from the Eastern Bus Terminal on Sukhumvit Road to Samut Prakan. Open: daily, 8am–5pm. Admission charge.

A keeper and his croc, Samut Prakan

CROCODILE FARM

Some 30,000 crocodiles are to be found at the kingdom's biggest farm, in Samutprakarn Province, 30km from Bangkok, performing shows when they are alive and sold as handbags when dead. Hourly shows, some featuring crocodile wrestling, take place. At other times you can watch them basking in the sun or semi-submerged in an ink-black lake.

Traditional Thai houses in the Ancient City

WHAT TO SEE

When you have had enough of crocodiles, there are plenty of other animals on show, including elephants, snakes, birds and monkeys, as well as a host of food stalls, picnic spots and other sundry amusements for children.
Location: 25km southeast of Bangkok near the town of Samut Prakan. Travel agents in Bangkok run half-day and full-day tours. Alternatively catch bus number 25 from the Eastern Bus Terminal on Sukhumvit Road to Samut Prakan. Open: daily, 7am–6pm. Admission charge.

DAMNOEN SADUAK

For a glimpse of the good old days when people traded from boats on canals, ignore the commercialised Thonburi Floating Market and instead take a tour to the small village of Damnoen Saduak.

From the first light of dawn the place is transformed into a watery market of diminutive paddlers. Traders, selling 10 different kinds of bananas, spiky durians, the king of all fruits, and tender grilled kebabs with chilli sauces, paddle around the canals while others barter in a deluge of colour that could come straight from a fairy-tale.

You can either watch the traders from along the walkways, where there is a land-based market selling handicrafts and coconuts, full of chasing dogs and smiling children, or you can take a boat tour from the Chang Pier near the Grand Palace and join the milling crowds on the water.

Most tours include a boat trip around the maze of canals, where the fruit and vegetables are brought in from all over the central plains region. Some excursions include a trip to a nearby snake farm.

Although the people of Damnoen Saduak have learned the value of tourism, with shops and boutiques catering to the coachloads of day trippers, the scenes of yesteryear are more than enough to make up for this. Most people leave with a film full of good pictures and some of their finest memories of Thailand.
Location: 109km to the southwest of Bangkok, reached by bus from Bangkok's Southern Bus Terminal via Nakhon Pathom. It is best to take a day tour, choosing one that gets you to the market in the early morning. Admission free.

Damnoen Saduak: popular with tourists

The bridge on the River Khwae

KANCHANA BURI

Mention the name Kanchana Buri and two visions come to mind: one of war and the other of peace and calm. For Kanchana Buri is both a beautiful province and the location of the Khwae Bridge, which was to become famous through Pierre Boulle's chilling novel and the subsequent film.

During World War II hundreds of thousands of prisoners were put to work on the bridge and railway, which was designed to connect Japanese-controlled Singapore with the Burmese capital, Rangoon. Many died of malaria, others from beatings, starvation and exhaustion.

Although part of the bridge was bombed in 1945, you can still see the original version (with its rebuilt central section). It spans the Khwae Yai river just 5km north of Kanchana Buri town and carries the railway from Bangkok to the town of Nam Tok (see page 34). Under the bridge, enterprising salesmen use their rafts as floating restaurants.

Getting there

Kanchana Buri is 130km west of Bangkok. A train leaves at 7.45am every day from Thonburi Railway Station taking 2 to 3 hours. Buses leave every 15 minutes from Bangkok's Southern Bus Terminal on Phra Pinklao Road. For the more up-market accommodation on the river, make reservations through Bangkok travel agents prior to departure.

War memorials

Victims of the war are remembered in two cemeteries and by a Japanese memorial. The Chung Kai War Cemetery lies on the banks of the Khwae Noi river, 20 minutes outside of town, and the Kanchana Buri War Cemetery is on Saeng Chuto Road, near the town's railway station.
On Paak Phraek Road there is also the Jeath War Museum. Open: 8.30am–4.30pm. Admission charge.

National Parks

Most people who come to Kanchana Buri these days do so for its other secrets: to enjoy the quiet surroundings,

WHAT TO SEE

to take river rafting trips on the Khwae or to explore the sapphire mines at Bo Phloi, 50km north.

More adventurous travellers or those with more time can use Kanchana Buri as a stepping stone to the town of Sangkhla Buri, 200km to the northwest, near the Burmese border, or the two nearby National Parks, the Erawan (72km north) and the Sai Yok (100km west), which offer beautiful unspoilt scenery and waterfalls.

There is no need to slum it either. Luxury developments along the way allow visitors to explore during the day and relax at night. Some of the raft complexes have restaurants and swimming pools. The River Kwai Village (tel: 591055) even has a zoo.

KHAO YAI NATIONAL PARK

Tigers and elephants may not be a common sight at Khao Yai, but they do exist, along with monkeys, black bears, Asian wild dogs and some of the kingdom's most colourful birdlife.

The nearest national park to Bangkok, Khao Yai ('Big Mountain') is also one of the kingdom's largest, with more than 2,000sq km of evergreen forest scattered with teak and mahogany. At weekends, the park gets extremely crowded and some of

You have been warned!

Facilities are good throughout Khao Yai

the wildlife understandably makes itself scarce. Warm clothes are recommended.

Visitors who are fortunate may come across great slaty woodpeckers and one of the highest concentrations of hornbills in the country. A network of paths cuts through much of the park and with the help of maps you can hike to the elephant watch tower and to the beautiful waterfalls of Heo Suwat and Heo Narok. Ideally, though, it is best to have a guide and transport. In the evening elephant-spotting tours are arranged by the national park lodge using spotlights to 'freeze' the animals.
Location: 198km from Bangkok. Thai State Railways organise one-day tours which leave Bangkok's Hualamphong Station at 6am and return the same evening, but you must book in advance. Khao Yai can also be reached by train and bus to Pak Chong, the nearest town, from where you must catch a songthaew *(truck taxi) to the park headquarters.*

RICE HARVEST

In early November, the fields of central Thailand turn from green to golden brown: villagers descend into the paddies and the crop, known to the Thais as *khao suai* or 'beautiful rice' is harvested. Every year Thailand grows over 20 million tonnes of rice, more than any other country in the world, and more than 50 per cent of the population participates in the harvest in some way.

Ploughing takes place with the aid of water buffalo or, in a few richer communities, with tractors. Once the labour is finished the fields are flooded by means of a complex series of irrigation channels leading from nearby rivers, streams and canals.

At this time, the rice seedlings are planted by hand. The rains begin and three months later the rice in the fields is ready for harvest. Once again villagers go out in large groups working with sickles. The cut rice is spread in the fields to dry for several days, then arranged in sheaves and taken to the family compound where it will be bought by wholesalers, to be sold, consumed and enjoyed in countries around the world.

Despite the backbreaking manual toil, most workers in the rice fields receive a very low wage – but it keeps the population from starving and, over the centuries, rice has probably been the biggest cause of stability in the kingdom.

Various stages of the rice harvest, after which the stubble is burnt off and the paddy can be planted once again

LOP BURI

The old town of Lop Buri is an amalgam of almost every chapter in Thailand's history. During the Dvaravati period (6th to 10th centuries), it was inhabited by Lavah people who called the town Lavo. In 950 it fell to the Khmers, who ruled it until the 13th century. During the 13th century, the shrewd kings of Ayutthaya established a second capital here in case their city fell to the warring Burmese. These days modern shopping arcades add to the spectrum of architectural styles.

... and their only inhabitants

Getting there
Lop Buri lies 154km north of Bangkok. Trains leave from Hualamphong Station 11 times a day taking 2½ hours. Buses leave regularly from the Northern Bus Terminal on Phahon Yothin Road.

Phra Narai Rajanivet
The highlight of Lop Buri for most visitors is this royal palace, former home to King Narai of Ayutthaya, one of the town's most intriguing characters. It was he who, in the 17th century, won the

The bleak Khmer ruins at Sam Yod ...

heart of Louis XIV's French emissaries and who even made Constantine Phaulkon, a Greek, his prime minister. Narai was finally usurped, but the huge battlemented walls, the ruins of the king's elephant stables and a small museum can still be seen.
Location: Sorasak Road. Open: Wednesday to Sunday, 9am–noon and 1–4pm. Admission charge.

Phraprang Sam Yod
Framed against the main line railway to Bangkok are the old Khmer ruins of Phraprang Sam Yod. The temple, named after its three impressive *prangs* (spires), typical of Lop Buri style, was built in the 13th century. Monkeys scamper around the nearby shrine of San Phra Karn.
Location: on Wichayen Road, near the railway track. Admission free.

Houseboats and markets
Other temples worth visiting are Wat Phra Sri Mahathat, a lofty, 12th-century Khmer temple situated opposite the railway station, and the Brahminic shrine of San Phra Kahn, next to the level crossing.

Two other things not to miss are the wooden houseboats on the river and the

WHAT TO SEE

nearby busy market selling fruits, flowers and beautiful woven baskets.

NAKHON PATHOM

There is only one reason to come to Nakhon Pathom, and that is to see the *chedi* (pagoda) which claims to be the tallest in the world. The *chedi*, which resembles an upturned ice-cream cornet, is over 120m high and is supposed to mark the place where Buddhism was first brought by Indian missionaries in the 3rd century BC.

The huge honey-coloured *chedi* was begun in 1853, during the reign of King Mongkut, when the much older *chedi* that lies within the big one underwent considerable renovation. Later the outer *chedi* was encased in gold-coloured tiles from China.

Nakhon Pathom is famous for fruit-growing; you may come across the famous *som-o* (pomelo), the luscious fruit that has become a staple of the provincial economy. It is harvested in August and November and sold throughout the country.

Location: 59km west of Bangkok. Trains leave from Hualamphong Railway Station 10 times a day taking 1½ hours. Buses leave every 20 minutes from the Southern Bus Terminal on Phra Pinklao Road from 6am–10.30pm. Day tours from Bangkok are generally combined with a trip to the floating market at Damnoen Saduak (see page 67).

ROSE GARDEN

Set in beautiful lush surroundings, the Rose Garden is designed for those who want a touch of calm and colour away from the city. Cultural shows begin daily at 3pm with a programme that includes Thai folk dancing, Thai boxing, cock-fighting and sword duels. There is also a swimming pool and the opportunity to go

Every tourist's aim in Thailand

boating or waterskiing. Some visitors find the place too commercialised, even by Thai standards, but nobody can complain about the tropical gardens themselves, located on the banks of the Thachin River with a nearby golf course and hotel.

Location: some 32km west of Bangkok. Trips can be arranged by contacting the Rose Garden Office in Bangkok (tel: 295 3261). Open: daily, 8am–6pm. Admission charge.

Northern Thailand

The umbrella factory of Chiang Mai

CHIANG MAI

Almost everyone visits Chiang Mai at some stage of their visit to Thailand, for the northern capital and the kingdom's second largest city appears to have everything that Bangkok does not: a life that is slower, a population that is more manageable and the feel more of a fast-developing province than of a major city.

That is not to say that Chiang Mai is provincial. Commercially it is now a thriving centre producing countless items which are exported worldwide. But the town has the unique advantage of a mountain setting, a cooler temperate climate and, during the months of spring, some of the most beautiful flowers that you will ever come across. Furthermore, it is a major staging post for trekking in the hill district and for visiting hilltribes, migrants from Burma and Laos, whose dress and handicrafts lure so many visitors from the west.

Chiang Mai itself is also the handicrafts centre of Thailand and the producer of fine lacquerware, ceramics, hilltribe clothes, jewellery and even opium pipes.

Even so, do not expect to see a totally unspoilt town. Chiang Mai changed a long time ago when the steady flow of admirers demanded an increase in hotels, guest houses, condominiums and shopping arcades. Still, for those in search of something a little different and who do not expect everything to be authentic, it still justifies the title 'Rose of the North' and is the most vibrant and convivial town in Thailand.

Legendary past

The Thais were latecomers to Chiang Mai. It was the Mons and the Khmers who first controlled the region through a string of principalities that lasted well into the 13th century.

Then came the turn of a Lanna chieftain named King Mengrai. Legend tells that he was riding along the banks of the Ping river in pursuit of an elephant when he noticed two white sambar deer, two white barking deer and five mice. Taking this as an auspicious sign he founded the city of Chiang Mai on this precise spot and then went on to expand the Kingdom of Lanna until it stretched all the way from the northern frontier of the Sukhothai Kingdom to the southern provinces of China.

In 1556, Chiang Mai and much of the north fell again to the Burmese who occupied the city on and off for almost 200 years. It was not until the late 1700s that the Thais regained control.

The latest people to leave a mark are property speculators, but even these are tied to ancient beliefs. Each property is started at an auspicious time to please the local spirits. And every year, festivals recall the legendary exploits of Lanna and the cultural integrity of a city which still quietly prides itself on its independence.

A place to wander

The city of Chiang Mai offers much to see and do. The town is easily negotiated by using the red truck taxis *(songthaews)* that endlessly circulate around the town. Alternatively you can explore on foot and hire a tricycle taxi or a *tuk tuk* when you are weary.

Getting there

Thai Airways International has daily flights from Bangkok to Chiang Mai taking one hour. Regular buses also leave the Northern Bus Terminal on Phahon Yothin Road, Bangkok, taking 11 hours. The most pleasant means of transport is the overnight sleeper that leaves Bangkok's Hualamphong Railway Station in the early evening and gets you to the kingdom of Lanna at dawn.

BANYEN FOLK ART MUSEUM

A charming little museum, Banyen also houses some of the finest antiques and woodcarvings in the city. It was started more than 30 years ago by a young tribeswoman who has since become one of the best-known collectors in the north. Even if you are not interested in purchasing, the leafy gardens and charming old traditional house are well worth a visit.

Location: off Wualai Road (tel: 274 007). Open: daily, Friday to Wednesday, 10am–4pm. Admission charge.

CHIANG MAI ZOO

Thailand's biggest zoo has about 500 species, a beautiful open-air bird sanctuary and was previously the private collection of Harold Young, an American working as an instructor with the Border Patrol Police.

Location: in a pretty area some 6km from town and best visited on the way to the mountain-top temple of Doi Suthep. Open: daily, 8am–5pm. Admission charge.

CULTURAL CENTRE

The place to go for northern style banqueting and dances. Inside the cultural centre made from reconstructed tribal houses, eat *khantoke* style dinners along with coachloads of other tourists.

Location: on 185/3 Wualai Road (Tel: 275 097). Open: nightly, 7–10pm. Reserve in advance.

NATIONAL MUSEUM

A vast Buddha's head, believed to have been part of one of the biggest bronzes ever cast in Thailand, is the chief attraction of Chiang Mai's National Museum. There are other things to see such as a massive Buddha footprint made from wood and mother-of-pearl, terracottas and ceramics. Folk and hilltribe arts and crafts are exhibited on the upper floor along with the bed of the former prince of Chiang Mai.

Location: north of Super Highway, to the northwest of town. Open: Wednesday to Sunday, 9am–noon and 1–4pm. Admission charge.

Food stall at a Bangkok market

NIGHT BAZAAR

Bangkok's pride at night may be Patpong but Chiang Mai's less flamboyant variety attracts just as many visitors. The so-called Night Bazaar consists of the three-storey mock-Tudor Chiang Mai Plaza and the Ying Ping Bazaar. Their combined boutiques sell everything from high fashion to tribal ware, antiques, pots, lacquerware, jewellery and leather. In some shops you can actually see cloths being woven into tribal ware. Outside, on the roadside, are stalls selling camera film, painted beetles, bracelets and fake designer T-shirts and watches, while near by there are hundreds of sizzling foodstalls.

Location: Chang Khlan Road. Open: 6pm–midnight. Remember to bargain

SAN KAMPHAENG ROAD

Someone should have nicknamed this 'Handicrafts Road', since the 15km stretch of tarmac that leads east of Chiang Mai to San Kamphaeng has become the biggest handicrafts market in the country, lined with emporia selling everything from silver and silk to woodcarvings and lacquerware.

This is the place to stock up on your presents and, more than anything, to watch village arts which in many places are now disappearing. Here you can see silk being made from silkworms fed on mulberry leaves, lacquerware being sprayed individually and umbrellas painted by hand. There is no charge for

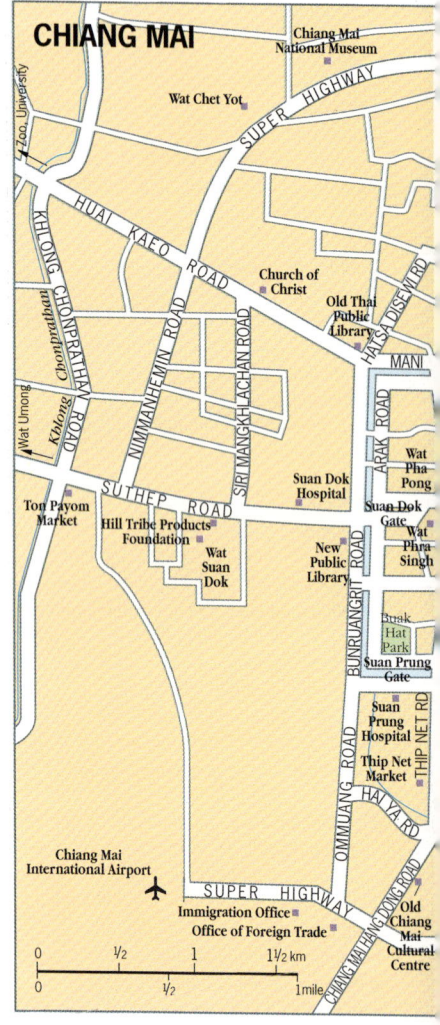

WHAT TO SEE

browsing and no need for tipping. Sometimes you can even order specially made items that will be shipped back home for you.

It is best to arrive early as coachloads of day trippers become an increasing feature in the afternoon. In the vicinity there are plenty of restaurants or shops for snacks or ice-cream.

Location: to the east of Chiang Mai along Highway 1006, reached by bus from Charoen Muang Road or by tuk tuk.

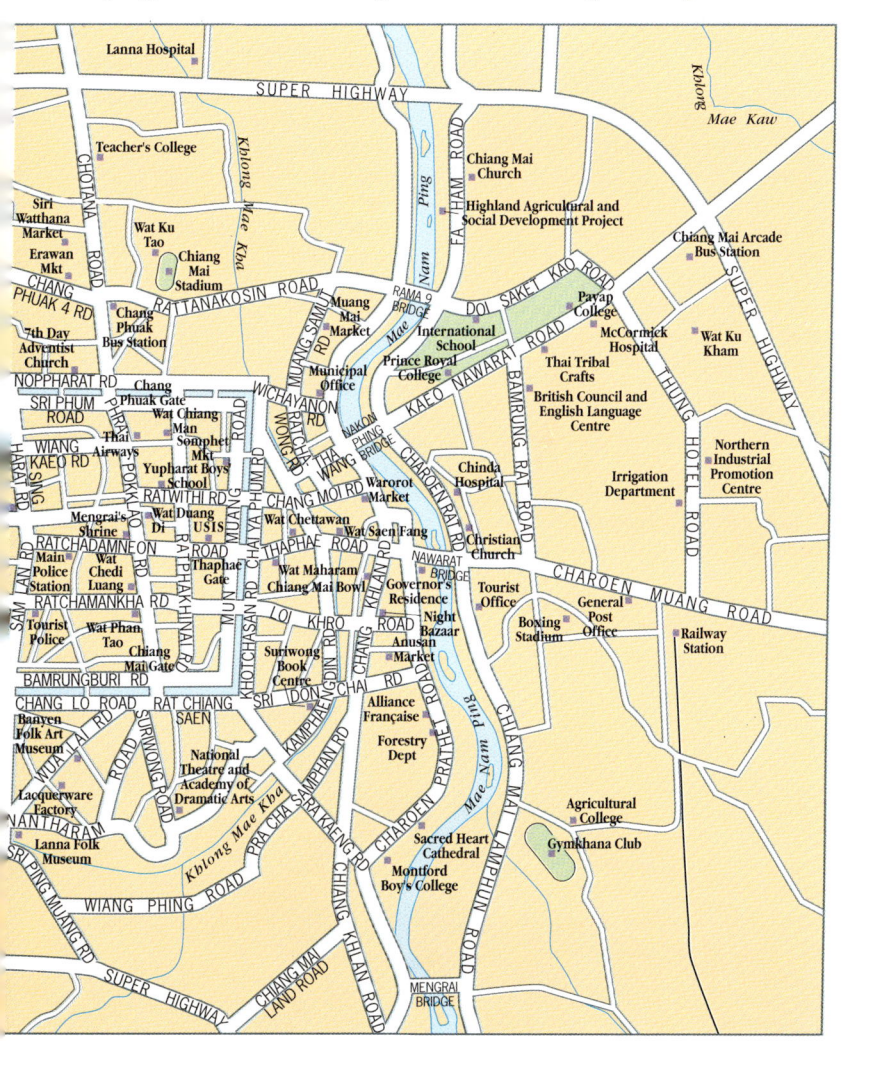

Chiang Mai's Temples

*W*ithin the vicinity of Chiang Mai lie more than 300 temples, almost all of them still in use. Those listed here can easily be seen together or in small doses as befits the mood. For a tricycle tour, see page 38. Alternatively catch a day-tour organised by a big hotel.

Wat Chiang Man
Chiang Mai's oldest temple built around 1296 AD, Wat Chiang Man was founded by Mengrai, the man who established the great Kingdom of Lanna and subsequently died there, struck by a bolt of lightning. Two figures are particularly revered and are believed to have supernatural powers.
Location: off Ratphakhinai Road within the walled city. Open: daily, 9am–5pm. Admission free.

Wat Chet Yot
Wat Chet Yot, known as the 'Temple of Seven Spires,' was built in the 15th century, during the reign of King Tilokaraja, to recall the great Mahabodi temple in Bodh Gaya (India), where Buddha achieved enlightenment. This is one of the most striking and important of the town's temples. Inside the larger *chedi* (pagoda) are the ashes of King Tilokaraja and outside two sacred *bo* trees, said to have come from the original one in the Kingdom of Sakyas in present-day Nepal.
Location: on the Super Highway off Huai Kaeo Road. Open: daily, 8am–5pm. Admission free.

Wat Ku Tao
This is one of the most striking and delightful temples you will come across, with its *chedi* (pagoda) shaped like five melons, intricately decorated with pieces of coloured porcelain. The structure, dating from 1613, is believed to represent five Buddhist monks' alms bowls which symbolise five Lord Buddhas. Note the striking sculptures

Wat Phra Singh contains some fine buildings as well as precious statues

on the outer walls.
Location: north of the moat near the Chiang Mai Sports Stadium. Admission free.

Wat Chedi Luang

It took an earthquake to shake the massive foundations of Wat Chedi Luang. The temple had been built in 1401 and enlarged to a height of 86m. An earthquake in 1545 left the *chedi* in ruins, but it has now been impressively restored.
Location: on Phra Pokklao Road, near the intersection with Ratchamankha Road. Open: daily, 8am–5pm. Admission free.

Wat Phra Singh

The 14th-century temple of Wat Phra Singh became the residence for one of the kingdom's most famous statues when a cart carrying the precious figure broke down on its way from Lampang. The Phra Singh image has since lost its original head; that was taken by thieves in 1922, but the replacement remains.
Location: at the intersection of Ratchadamnoen and Sing Harat Road. Open: daily, 8am–5pm. Admission free.

Wat Suan Dok

This is the perfect spot to be at sunset with the three ancient *chedis* (pagodas) framed against the hills in the distance. Wat Suan Dok ('the Flower Garden Temple') was built by King Ku Na in 1383, within the pleasure gardens of the monarchs of Lanna Thai, and it contains a large 500-year-old bronze image of Buddha in Chiang Saen style. Most of the royals of Chiang Mai are buried in the cemetery adjoining the temple, although several of the *chedis* also contain their ashes. One is even said to contain an important relic of the Buddha brought here by elephant.

The new Wat Phra Singh

Location: off Cherng Doy Road, south of Suthep Road, on the western outskirts of town. Open: daily, 8am–5pm. Admission free.

Wat Umong

Away from the other temples, in the relative quiet of the edge of town, Wat Umong is more like a monastic retreat than a traditional *wat*. It was built by King Mengrai for a famous monk who could not stay in the city since he had to practice the Lord Buddha's teaching in a peaceful environment. Inside the grounds are cells for meditation and attached to the trees are tablets advising people that 'today is better than two tomorrows'. In the past several foreign monks have resided here.
Location: in the western outskirts, reached by taking the Suthep Road, shortly beyond the junction with Khlong Chonprathan Road, take the turning to the left signposted to the wat which is reached after 1km. Admission free.

CHIANG MAI ENVIRONS

DOI INTHANON
Thailand's tallest mountain cannot compare with the Himalayas, but at 2,599m above sea level, it still offers fine views of the surrounding national park. From along the steep road that runs all the way from the park entrance to the top of Doi Inthanon, walks can be taken to caves and hilltribe villages, although you should get maps or hire guides from the park headquarters. Birdwatchers especially may be rewarded. The park has one of the highest concentrations of birdlife including the rare ashy-throated warbler and the yellow-bellied flowerpecker.

On the way up, visit the Mae Klang Waterfall, signposted outside the park gates and especially spectacular during the rainy months from August to November.
Location: Doi Inthanon lies 80km southwest of Chiang Mai. Tours are generally the best way of seeing the park, since buses only go as far as Chom Thong from where you will have to catch another to Mae Klang and from there take a songthaew *(truck taxi) to Doi Inthanon. Alternatively, use private transport. Accommodation is available.*

DOI SUTHEP
High up an exciting road that zigzags its way up the mountainside is the revered temple of Doi Suthep, which dates from 1383. Legend has it that the temple was established at the spot where one of the king's own white elephants fled the palace, climbed to the summit, trumpeted three times and died. Centuries later pious volunteers constructed a road there, with people coming from as far as Lampang to contribute to the endeavours.

You cannot go the full way on four wheels though. The road curves around near the base of the hill and visitors must still either take the arduous 290-step climb up a Naga staircase or a 4-minute ride on the mountain railway.

At the top is a monastery with bells and gold umbrellas and rows of Buddhas marking the spot where important relics are encased. On a clear day, you may catch fine views of Chiang Mai.
Location: 15km west of Chiang Mai. Minibuses regularly leave from the Chang Phuak (White Elephant) Gate, on the northern edge of Chiang Mai's moat. Most people take tours.

PHU PHING PALACE
Four kilometres up the road from Doi Suthep is the Phu Phing Palace, the royal winter residence of the king, with its sumptuous gardens.
Open: Friday to Sunday, except when the family is in residence.

TRIBAL VILLAGE OF BAN DOI PUI
Another popular side trip is to the tribal village of Ban Doi Pui. The village is inhabited by the Hmong (or Meo), an ethnic tribe characterised by their colourful costumes and their love of opium. This village provides little in the way of authenticity, but it does give a sense of the colour and of the traditions that once shaped these people before the advent of tourism.
Location: 8km from Doi Suthep and 4km from Phu Phing Palace. Trips to the Hmong village are combined with tours to Doi Suthep.

LAMPANG
An old timber-cutting town and a former staging post on the journey up north, Lampang was, during the 7th century, an

WHAT TO SEE

outlying settlement of the Haripunchai empire. These days its biggest claim to fame is that horse-drawn carts remain a popular form of transport.

One sight not to be missed is Wat Phra Kaeo Don Tao, the temple near the banks of the Wang river which is once said to have housed the famous Emerald Buddha. Smaller typically Burmese temples, such as Wat Sri Chum and Wat Pha Fang, are also worth exploring.

One last gem for the real temple fanatic is the beautiful Wat Phra That Lampang Luang, some 16km to the south of the town, sporting fine bronzes and woodwork as well as an Emerald Buddha image said to have been cut from the same stone as the original now in Bangkok.

Location: 99km south of Chiang Mai. Buses run from the Chiang Mai Arcade station taking 1½ hours. The town is also on the main railway line linking Bangkok and Chiang Mai.

The revered temple of Doi Suthep

LAMPHUN

A 30-minute drive from Chiang Mai, along a road lined with majestic trees, will bring you to another old historical city, once the capital of the great kingdom of Haripunchai. Lamphun was founded in 660 by Queen Chama Devi and remained the capital until 1281, when the empire fell under the sovereignty of King Mengrai, monarch of the Lanna dynasty.

No visitor to the town should miss the temple complex of Wat Phra That Haripunchai, on Highway II, originally founded in 1044, and bearing two ornamental lions and two fine bronze Buddha statues.

A couple of other sights deserve a mention. Wat Ku Kut (commonly known as Wat Chama Devi), on the western side of town towards Sanphathong village, dates from the 8th century, although the present buildings are modern. Opposite Wat Phra That Haripunchai, there is also the small national museum (open Wednesday to Sunday, 9am–4pm) with a collection of sculptures from the Dvaravati, Haripunchai and Lanna periods.

If you have got the time, take a *songthaew* (truck taxi) to the town of Pa Sang which lies 11km to the southwest. This is famed for its *longans* (a fruit resembling a lychee), its handicrafts and, above all, its beautiful women.

Location: 26km south of Chiang Mai, reached by regular bus from Lamphun Road near Nawarat Bridge.

MAE SA VALLEY

Everything that tourists associate with the north is on offer in Mae Sa, a lush valley that has become a showpiece of local cultural and natural attractions.

Orchid cultivation, elephants, butterfly farms, snake farms, waterfalls: they are all to be found here along with quaint resorts and hilltribe centres.

The place is especially good for children who wish to see things without too much traipsing around, but it is thoroughly commercialised and has to be taken with a pinch of salt.

Location: 15km north of Chiang Mai. Day tours or private transport is the best bet since buses only go as far as Mae Rim.

MAE TAENG

The name of Mae Taeng is associated with Thailand's most beloved four-legged animal: the *chang*, or elephant, was, until recently, found not only in the forests of the north but also in the king's palace in Bangkok where it was frequently consulted on important matters of state. The elephants of Mae Taeng are, however, just reminders of a sight once common throughout the country. Elephants were then used to drag logs to the river where they would be floated downstream. The use of elephants has diminished over the

Over 1,000 species of orchid are found in Thailand

WHAT TO SEE

Working elephants enjoy their daily bath

centuries and they are now used mainly for tourist displays.

Daily shows, however, bring to life an era that is no more. Mahouts show the skill and adaptability of their massive steeds and elephant rides provide visitors with the feel and smell of these obliging beasts. Raft trips are also arranged through the leafy woodlands around the park.

Location: 60km north of Chiang Mai. Day trips are organised by travel agencies. Alternatively catch a bus leaving from the Chang Phuak Terminal on Chotana Road in the direction of Fang and ask for the Elephant Training Centre. Open: daily, 9am–12.30pm. Admission charge.

ORCHIDS GALORE

Thailand's most famous flower is the orchid. The kingdom grows some 1,000 different varieties, making it one of the most prolific producers in the world. Some of the most famous orchids are 'Queen Sirikit', *Paphiopedium ascocenda* and 'Miss Udorn Sunshine', all renowned for their subtle fragrance and their elegance. The best place to see them is in the orchid farms around Chiang Mai and in the Mae Sa Valley. But even in Bangkok, in the early morning markets and stalls, Thailand's favourite flower can be appreciated.

People of the northern hills:
the Akha, young and old

The Lisu

The Lahu,
who come as far
south as Tak

HILLTRIBES

They live in the northern hills, high up near the borders in the area known as the Golden Triangle, the wilderness of land that lies at the point where the borders of Laos, Thailand and Burma meet. They wear strange colourful clothes and worship the spirits of the hills and the rains.

The hilltribe population of Thailand numbers some 550,000, made up of the Akha, Karen, Lahu, Lisu, Hmong (Meo) and Mien. Each tribe comes from a different ancestral home, wears a different costume and has distinctive attitudes towards the spirits, to marriage, to sickness and to wealth.

Traditionally these people tilled the soil, growing opium, maize or potatoes, high up in the barren hills and migrating when the soil was turned over to fallow. Many came from over the Thai border, crossing freely between countries, settling on the fringes of northern Thailand and moving on.

Time has gradually eroded their values as the modern world has caught up. Some tribespeople have become farmers, having moved down to the plains, while others have given up their tribal clothes for the dream of jeans, a T-shirt and a life in the city.

Even so, the majority of tribespeople still preserve at least some of their traditions, eking out an existence that appears, from the outside, to be idyllic, though in reality it is a hard life tied to the soil, the family spirits and the home.

The long-necked Karen

Chiang Rai's Wat Phra Kaeo

CHIANG RAI

The northernmost capital of Chiang Rai is one of the oldest towns in Thailand. Now, despite the many modern hotels catering for the growing influx of tourists, there is still something rather provincial about the place. Although there are only a limited number of sights, Chiang Rai's biggest attractions lie in the surrounding countryside, with the town's hotels and restaurants merely serving for those beginning or ending their journey there.

Most people come here for trekking trips, ranging from one-day packages in buses to five days on elephants and rafts. You only need walk down the main street to find something tailored to your price range and desired degree of comfort.

A wild elephant

If it were not for an elephant that ran wild, Chiang Rai might never have been established at all. As legend recalls, it was only this which attracted King Mengrai to the auspicious site where he founded the city in 1262. For a short spell Chiang Rai served as the capital of the Lanna kingdom but it was rapidly eclipsed by the growth of Chiang Mai. It fell to the Burmese in the 16th century and became a jungle backwater close to the border areas where the tribes and the drug smugglers ruled supreme.

Thus it remained until the present day when Chiang Rai began to expand as Chiang Mai began to feel the constraints of excessive growth.

Getting there

Chiang Rai is 182km north of Chiang Mai. Near by are the towns of Doi Mae Salong, Mae Sai, Chiang Saen and the Golden Triangle.

Chiang Rai is reached from Chiang Mai by river (see below), by regular buses, taking four hours, or by aeroplane, taking 40 minutes.

River journey

One of the greatest highlights of a visit to Chiang Rai may well prove to be the journey there and back from Chiang Mai, since part of the trip is by boat and passes through some of the most spectacular scenery in the region.

To do the trip you must catch a bus or *songthaew* (truck taxi) to Tha Ton, a little settlement which lies five hours due north of Chiang Mai, on the banks of the Kok river. From here boats leave at around noon daily for the five-hour trip to Chiang Rai. The long-tailed boats are fast and uncomfortable, with engines that sound like thunder, and no toilet. Any short-term discomforts are made up for by the countryside and the views of hills, villages and countless water buffalo. Rafts can also be rented for a slower three-day journey to Chiang Rai, although you are well advised to make advance reservations.

Temples
Chiang Rai's most famous temple is the 13th-century **Wat Phra Kaeo** on Trairat Road, home to a model of the Emerald Buddha. To the west of Wat Phra Kaeo, situated on a small hill, is **Wat Doi Tong**, with fine views of the river and the distant hills beyond. *Open: daily, 8.30am–6pm. Admission free.*

Tribes and elephants
One popular side trip is to the tribal village of Ban Ruammit on the banks of the Kok river. The Karen tribespeople here are no strangers to tourism, yet most visitors enjoy the elephant rides and the journey there. A long-tailed boat leaves daily from the pier near the Dusit Resort; the journey takes one hour, but you must return by minibus.

Further afield are the towns of Mae Chan, 32km north, and Mae Salong, 67km northwest, far enough away to get a real feel of the countryside and its isolation, but near enough for luxury and a touch of homely comforts. Both can be reached by bus and organised tours.

A colourful girl of the Lisu tribe

Take an early morning trip down the Kok river from Chiang Rai to get away from it all

You can cross the bridge at Mae Sai into Burma

THE GOLDEN TRIANGLE

No other area in Thailand conjures up such images as the Golden Triangle, the evocative-sounding region that lies to the north of Chiang Rai at the point where the great rivers Mekong and Ban Sop Ruak meet to form the apex of Thailand, Laos and Burma.

It is little wonder the region gained its legendary infamy. Since the 1960s, it has become the largest supplier of opium in the world as well as home to drug armies and to Khun Sa, the ineffable 'Prince of Poppies' a Shan warlord fighting the Burmese government.

Pinpointing the exact location of the triangle was largely irrelevant until the tourist authorities ingeniously found a spot for it. Now there is a big plaque opposite a sandbank at Ban Sop Ruak, a range of over-priced boat trips and countless stalls selling Golden Triangle T-shirts.

Most people who come here are invariably disappointed. It is far better to explore the surrounding countryside or the thriving towns of Mae Sai and Chiang Saen.

The Golden Triangle is centred on the town of Ban Sop Ruak, some 40km north of Chiang Rai.

Mae Sai

The chief town nearest to the official Golden Triangle is Mae Sai. It lies about as far north as you can go in Thailand. The town hugs the banks of the Mae Sai river, a jumble of wooden houses, concrete shops and corrugated shacks bisected by a long road and an austere concrete bridge leading to Burma.

Every day, from 6am to 6pm, the

OPIUM

Papaver somniferum is the innocuous Latin name of the poppy that produces one of the world's most dangerous drugs. It is found in the resin of the poppy, is extracted by hand and is turned into heroin in refineries along the Thai border.

Every year more than 2,000 tonnes comes over from the Golden Triangle, shipped, flown and smuggled to destinations around the world. Some of it is distributed in the big cities of Thailand and some is used by the local tribes, many of whom have become addicts of the drug.

Whilst recent efforts have led to a reduction of opium cultivation in Thailand, the flow of drugs from the bordering countries continues. Even with the introduction of alternative crops, the massive amounts of money involved in trafficking makes any attempt to kill the drug trade mere wishful thinking.

WHAT TO SEE

Deadly opium from these beautiful and innocuous-looking poppies ...

bridge is the scene of frenzied shopping, for this is the main border crossing; bring a camera and take some time.

Afterwards try shopping for gems or woven Burmese carpets or herbs in the market or along the main road which leads down from the bridge. Many of the beautiful *sequens* (mother-of-pearl buttons) and puppets are of such quality that they draw buyers from as far afield as Bangkok.

But where there are bargains, there are inevitably fakes and many jewel

... is smoked by many of the hill tribes

buyers may find themselves bearing away little more than coloured pieces of glass.

Location: 68km north of Chiang Rai and is reached by frequent buses taking 1½ hours. A VIP bus leaves daily from Bangkok (contact local travel agents).

Chiang Saen

Chiang Saen has something of a history, a little bit of intrigue and a great deal of calm. It lies just a few steps from the border with Laos, on the Mekong and 11km from Ban Sop Ruak.

Founded in the 14th century by the Mengrai dynasty, the town went on to become the centre of one of the earliest northern principalities. Reminders of those days can still be found in the old moat that surrounds the town, the fascinating museum (open Wednesday to Sunday, 9am–4pm) situated near the city gate, and Wat Pa Sak (the 'Teak Forest Temple') with its magnificent stuccoed *chedi* (pagoda) which predates the town.

Location: 48km northeast of Chiang Rai. Chiang Saen can be reached by bus from Chiang Rai and Mae Sai.

MAE HONG SON

Mae Hong Son (City of Mists) lies in a deep valley surrounded by hills, at the end of a staggeringly beautiful eight-hour drive from Chiang Mai or a more bearable 30-minute flight. If Chiang Mai has a central location to recommend it, Mae Hong Son is all about a sense of isolation, green hills and misty mornings. The town was only accessible by elephant until the early part of the century. Indeed, until a few years back, there was not even an airport. Now Mae Hong Son has the advantage of road and air connections and the comfort of good hotels.

Its few main streets pack in a fair amount of things to see, including temples, a picturesque lake and a morning market. Yet the real tonic is the scenic backdrop, the distant views and the mountain air.

If you are coming between November and February, remember to bring a sweater. Mae Hong Son can be bitterly cold, with temperatures at night falling to as low as 5°C (40°F).

Getting there

Mae Hong Son is situated 270km northwest of Chiang Mai. Nearby towns are Mae Sariang, 168km south, Pai, 102km east and Soppong, 57km northeast.

Buses to Mae Hong Son leave from Chiang Mai's Arcade Bus Station; those going via Pai taking 7 to 8 hours and those taking the more difficult route, via Mae Sariang, take 8 to 9 hours. A better alternative is the 30-minute Thai Airways International flight.

Morning market

You can still occasionally see some of the local tribespeople visiting the morning

> **SHANS**
>
> Until 1831, when the king of Chiang Mai sent out an expedition in search of elephants, Mai Hong Son's history remained as misty as its valleys. The abundance of four-legged animals, however, soon changed that and by 1874 a man named Phraya Singhanatdraja had been appointed as resident ruler.
>
> Members of the Burmese Shan tribe took this as a good example and rapidly settled there; thus the town grew, so much so that the Shans now constitute a majority of the province's population.

market. Try to get there at dawn because by 8am most people have packed up and gone home.

Location: behind the Mae Tee Hotel on Panetwattana Road

Soppong and Pai

For the adventurous, trips can be made to the beautiful Tham Lot Cave 68km away near Soppong, or to the small mountain village of Pai, which lies 45km further east. Both are situated in beautiful countryside and are easily reached by bus.

Alternatively there are now several organisations renting out motorbikes, or in some cases jeeps. If you hire a bike, be very careful: driving conditions are difficult, the roads are steep and foreigners with bandaged ankles and an embarrassed look are numerous.

Tham Pla

This is Mae Hong Son's most popular and easily reached sight. Tham Pla (Fish Cave) contains large and overweight carp fed on peanuts by visitors hoping to win

Be adventurous and take yourself for a day-trip to the stunning cave of Tham Lot

merit. Some people find it disappointing, but children love it.
Location: 18km north of town on road to Pai.

Trekking and tribes
Another of Mai Hong Son's specialities is the trip to the long-necked tribe, known as the Padang, who live in a village close to the Burmese border, reached by daily tours.

Mae Hong Son is also a good place to arrange trekking or to go elephant riding or rafting along the Pai river. Enquire at travel agents.

Wat Chong Klong and Wat Chong Kam
The most picturesque of Mae Hong Son's temples, on the banks of the charming Chong Kam Lake. They are best visited in the morning when the lake is veiled by mist.
Location: off Chumnan Sathit Road to the south of town. Both open: daily. Admission free.

Wat Hua Wiang
This is an incongruous wooden temple that would look more at home in Nepal than in Thailand. It contains a highly venerated bronze Buddha statue which was cast in Burma.
Location: on Panetwattana Road next to the market. Open: daily, 8am–6pm. Admission free.

Wat Phra That Doi Kong Mu
On the hill above the town, are the two *chedis* (pagodas) of the 19th-century Wat Phra That Doi Kong Mu, built under the rule of the first governor. They are reached by the wise via a winding road and by the energetic after a steep climb.

Ancient Wat Chang Lom in Si Satchanalai

SUKHOTHAI

The 'Dawn of Happiness', the chapter of history which ushered in one of Thailand's greatest civilisations, began in the town of Sukhothai, the ancient kingdom that lies almost midway between Bangkok and Chiang Mai.

The Sukhothai period lasted less than 150 years (from 1238 to 1376) but is considered a golden age of Thai art and religion, producing some of the greatest monuments.

These ruins are spread over an area of 45sq km and are best seen by taking a tour of the historical park (see page 42) or by hiring a guide to indicate the most important monuments.

Getting there

Sukhothai lies 427km north of Bangkok. To the east is the major provincial town of Phitsanulok, 50km away, and to the west are the towns of Tak, 80km away, and Mae Sot, 160km away.

Sukhothai can be reached by bus from Bangkok's Northern Bus terminal on Phahon Yothin Road. Alternatively, catch a train from Bangkok's Hualamphong Railway Station to Phitsanulok, the nearest provincial town, from where it is an hour's journey to Sukhothai by bus.

Historical park

Almost all the major sights are situated within the historical park west of the town. Three temples, in particular, should not be missed.

Wat Mahathat is the largest temple, built in the 13th century and containing 198 *chedis* (pagodas). **Wat Sri Chum** is situated outside the northwest corner of the city and contains a gigantic seated Buddha, each finger of the statue being as tall as a man. **Wat Si Sawai** is a beautiful Khmer-style temple built in the 13th century with a picturesque moat.

Outside the city walls, some 3km to the west, are the temples of **Wat Saphin Hin** and **Wat Chang Rob**, wilder, less visited and best seen by hiring a bicycle.

One other sight worth visiting is the **Ramkamhaeng Museum** containing a

---

THE PERFECT BUDDHA

The most beautiful, serene and perfect Buddhas were those that evolved during the Sukhothai period. They are distinguished by their broad shoulders, elongated limbs and by their delicate oval faces. Many of the Buddhas are made from stucco and bronze, cast with unsurpassed craftmanship. They leave behind them an air of radiant calm, an air that few artistic pieces have so powerfully and yet pervasively created.

replica of the famous Ramkamhaeng inscription: 'There is rice in the fields. Those who want to laugh can laugh, those who want to cry can cry.'
Ramkamhaeng Museum open: Wednesday to Sunday, 9am–4pm. Admission charge. Location: the Historical Park lies 13km from new Sukhothai and is easily reached by songthaew *(truck taxi). Open: daily until dusk. Admission charge.*

Si Satchanalai

An hour's drive north from Sukhothai, beyond a chequerboard of rice and tapioca fields, is the old walled city of Si Satchanalai. Wilder, more compact and for the most part less visited, it contains a wealth of temples, although on a smaller scale than in Sukhothai.

Wat Chang Lom is Si Satchanalai's most impressive monument. It dates from the 13th century and contains a large bell-shaped *chedi* (pagoda) raised on a square base decorated with 39 elephant buttresses.

Wat Chedi Chet Thaew is situated opposite Wat Chang Lom. This 14th-century temple houses seven rows of *chedis* said to contain the ashes of the city's rulers.

Wat Kah Phanom Phloeng is reached via a steep flight of stairs. The temple contains a seated Buddha and commands fine views of the ruins below.
Location: the old walled city is situated 5km south of the new town of Si Satchanalai. It can be reached by a bus that leaves Sukhothai every hour. Open: daily, 8.30am –4.30pm. Admission charge.

Ban Ko Noi

Outside the walled city, near the town of Ban Ko Noi, you can visit the kilns which produced some of Thailand's earliest and most beautiful pottery. Such was the value of the grey-green porcelain, known as Sawankalok, that examples have even been discovered as far afield as the Indonesian islands of Borneo and Sumatra.
Location: 4km north of Si Satchanalai. Open: daily, 9am–4pm. Admission charge.

A Buddha keeps watch at Wat Mahathat

Northeast Thailand

KHORAT (NAKHON RATCHASIMA)

The Thais call their town Nakhon Ratchasima, although most foreigners know it better as Khorat. The confusion over names, along with the lack of infrastructure and the rarity of English-speaking natives are enough to put off all but the persevering. That, however, can be part of the attraction. People do not come to Khorat to see the town; they come here as a springboard for some of the greatest ruins in the country.

Even so, everyone passing through should try to visit the night market on Manat Road as well as the statue of the famous Khun Ying Mo, the revered local who, during the reign of Rama III, saved the town from the Laotians. The statue is situated at the Chumpon Gate on the west side of town.

Getting there

The town of Khorat lies 259km northeast of Bangkok at the entrance to the Khorat Plateau. Nearby major towns are Buri Ram 150km east and Surin, 197km east. Khao Yai National Park is 99km to the west.

Trains run to Khorat seven times daily from Hualamphong Railway Station in Bangkok, taking approximately 5½ hours. Regular buses leave from Bangkok's Northern Bus Terminal in Phahon Yothin Road.

ANCIENT RUINS OF PHI MAI

One of the world's true wonders, the 11th-century temple at Phi Mai has not become a tourist attraction without good reason. It lies just an hour's journey north of Khorat by bus and just 240km from Angkor Wat, the famous Cambodian temple to which it was once connected by road. The central *prasad* (tower) alone is one of the tallest in Thailand, elaborately surrounded by four porches etched with intricate sandstone carvings of *nagas* and *garudas,* the mythical guardians of the temple.

Although the temple reached its peak during the reign of the Angkor monarch, Jayavarman VII (1181–1201), it fell into ruin and has only recently been restored to its former glory.

From Phi Mai, most people take the chance to visit a giant banyan tree called Sai Ngam, situated 2km down the road.
Location: 69km northeast of Khorat. Buses leave the main bus station on Suranari Road every half hour during the day.

MUANG TAM

This 10th-century temple is another beautiful example of Khmer architecture with three ancient ponds within its walled compound. Muang Tam is less visited, wilder and surrounded by the true countryside of Issan, a just reward for those who have made the effort to get there.
Location: 7km south of Phanom Rung (see opposite).

PAK THONG CHAI

Anyone coming to northeast Thailand should spend at least half a day exploring the region's two most famous commodities: silk and *mutmee. Mutmee* especially is associated with the northeast and is a unique form of tie-dyed silk

WHAT TO SEE

whereby the threads are tied according to the desired pattern before being dyed. Shops in Khorat sell fabulous quality silk. You can also watch the weavers at their looms in the nearby town of Pak Thong Chai.

Location: Pak Thong Chai lies 30km to the southwest of Khorat. The town is reached by bus that leaves Khorat every 30 minutes.

THE KHMERS

From the 8th to the 11th century vast areas of northeast Thailand were inhabited by the Khmers, a people who came from Cambodia.

Although they were gradually displaced by the Thais, they left behind them ruined temples dedicated to Khmer gods and to Buddha, which have a raw power found in few other artistic periods in Thai history.

The carvings at the ruins of 11th-century Phi Mai demonstrate the supreme artistry of the powerful Khmer people

PHANOM RUNG

Another fine example of Khmer architecture, Phanom Rung is solemnly perched on top of an extinct volcano. It is reached by a dramatic avenue paved with laterite, flanked by sandstone pillars, with ascending levels and three magnificent bridges carved with mythical beasts called *nagas*. The Khmers believed that the nearer to the sky a shrine was situated, the closer to the gods it would be. As a result, the shrine of Phanom Rung is considered especially sacred.

Location: 101km southeast of Khorat. You can take a bus from Khorat to Ban Ta Ko (bus terminal 2, bus number 274) from where, with luck, you will catch a songthaew *(truck taxi). A better bet is to take a tour.*

Embarking ferryboats to cross the river: some local people navigate the mighty Nam Khong many times a day

LOEI PROVINCE

The lure of Loei is its mountains, its waterfalls and its lush forest. The region, accessible only by a long road journey, is considered to be the Siberia of Thailand.

In reality it is one of the undiscovered gems of the northeast, calm and quiet with some of the greatest national parks in the country.

Getting there

Loei town is situated 520km northeast of Bangkok. Buses leave the Northern Bus Terminal on Phahon Yothin Road several times a day and the journey takes 10 hours.

CHIANG KHAN

On the Mekong river, almost on the border with Laos, is the small town of Chiang Khan set in a valley amidst rolling hills. Five kilometres downstream are the Kaeng Khut Khu Rapids. The town is favoured for its relative isolation and pleasant views.
Location: 45km north of Loei town and can be reached by songthaew *(truck taxi) from Loei bus station.*

NONG KHAI

The most popular town in the northeast, Nong Khai owes this position as much to its accessibility by rail as to its delightful river setting and proximity to Laos.

Long, tree-lined boulevards stretch along the banks of the Mekong river from whose cafés you can watch boats leave for the tiny Laotian border village

WHAT TO SEE

of Tha Dua. You can also eat French *baguette* (bread) in the markets and, at night, stare out at the twinkling lights of Vientiane, capital of the former French colony which fell to the Communists in 1975 and which is only now slowly re-emerging from its long self-imposed isolation.

On the outskirts of town, visit Wat Po Chai, site of the annual rocket festival, and the bizarre Brahmin complex of Wat Khaek, about 5km to the east.
Location: 614km northeast of Bangkok. Trains leave Hualamphong Station three times daily taking 10 hours. Buses run from the Northern Bus Terminal, Phahon Yothin Road taking nine hours.

THE MEKONG RIVER

From high up on the Tibetan plateau, the great Mekong river, the 12th longest river in the world, runs down for some 4,500km, snaking its way through China, Burma, Thailand and Laos before emptying out into the Mekong Delta of South Vietnam.

Along the way, it irrigates vast areas of land, supporting villages with rice, coconut, sugar cane and fish, providing miners with small finds of gold and vast communities with hydro-electric power.

At two points the Mekong forms the border between Thailand and Laos. In the dry season people can walk across the riverbed into Laos. At the northern-most point the Mekong cuts the area known as the Golden Triangle and for a long stretch extends through most of northeast Thailand. More than anything, the legendary Mekong is seen as a symbol of hope and unity among the disparate governments of Indo-China.

PHU KRADUNG

Sitting on a plateau 1,316m high is this weird and wonderful bell-shaped mountain that local people believe was made by spirits.

Access to Phu Kradung is not for the unfit. The park is reached by a steep path that winds its way up the hill. Guides do the journey in two hours and often carry baggage. The less fit should allow at least four or five hours.

From the top of the plateau you may catch glimpses of wild pigs or giant squirrels and, if you are lucky, elephants. More common are the unparalleled views of the plateau from Pha Nok Aen at dawn shrouded in mist.
Location: 72km south of Loei. Daily buses run from Loei to Phu Kradung. Check with the tourist office before setting off as during the rainy months especially (July to October) the national park is very often closed.

PHU LUANG NATIONAL PARK

Adventurous travellers can head for the Phu Luang Park, set high up on a plateau amidst magnificent scenery southwest of Loei. To see the reserve, you must get permission from the Loei Administration and Service Office *(tel: (042) 841 144)*, who provide guided tours, preferably to groups of 10 or more.

It's best to be fit to visit Phu Kradung

THE PEOPLE OF ISSAN

Scenes from Issan life: 'fishing' in a drained paddy

A water buffalo market

A village dance

In the alternately wet and arid squares of land that make up the vast canvas of northeast Thailand live the people of Issan, the 20 million farmers, rice workers and traders who have made this their home. Poor, isolated, tied to their soil, they are the poor and underprivileged of the kingdom.

Many Issan people are from Khmer stock or from Laos. Facially they are different from Thais, their skin darker, their physiques smaller and wirier. Linguistically they speak a language more akin to Khmer or Laotian. For many of them Bangkok is another world and the nextdoor village as far as their travels will ever take them.

Life in Issan is hard. When the rains fail, the people of Issan face the prospect of drought and famine. Many times the younger people of Issan have been forced to leave their homes, to seek work and wealth in the big cities, in Khorat or Bangkok. Few of them find what they are looking for, but rarely do they return. In their simple enduring smiles, their generosity and their legendary kindness, they reflect the real spirit of Issan, the spirit which suffers silently, but never gives up.

A water buffalo market

Cows on their way to pasture

SURIN

Surin is associated, in almost everyone's minds, with elephants – elephants playing football, elephants jousting or elephants holding a tug-of-war contest. This is largely thanks to the Thai Tourist Authority which in 1960 decided to host the first elephant round-up festival. So popular was the event that the two-day festival, held in the third week of November, has become an annual feature.

Outside of that time there are still good reasons to visit the town which is a picturesque provincial capital and typically Issan. Trips to Prasat Phra Viharn, the great 11th-century ruined Khmer temple situated over the border in Cambodia, can now be arranged through travel agents in Surin, although you should check first with the tourist authority in Bangkok *(tel: 226 0060)*.

One thing not to miss in Surin is the morning market, in the centre of the town, where you can eat *larb kwai* (spicy minced water-buffalo meat) and other inexpensive culinary delicacies made by a people renowned for their love of chillies. Here you can sit for hours simply absorbing the provincial feel, the dustiness, the heat and the raw nerve of Issan. When it is time to go, just point at your plate and smile, and they will bring a bill.

Getting there

Surin lies 456km northeast of Bangkok. Trains leave Hualamphong Railway Station 9 times daily taking seven hours. Buses run from the Northern Bus Terminal on Phahon Yothin Road several times daily. If coming during the

Bronze age artefacts, original ...

WHAT TO SEE

elephant festival, make sure you make a hotel reservation well in advance.

Hin Ban Pluang
Near Prasat, 38km to the south of Surin, is the 11th-century temple of Hin Ban Pluang, built to honour the Hindu god Vishnu. It is smaller and not as beautiful as the other Khmer-style temples in Thailand, but is certainly worth a visit for those who do not have the opportunity to see these other masterpieces.
Location: Hin Ban Pluang is signposted 5km from Prasat and is best reached by tour or private transport.

Silk Village
The native silk village of Khawowsinrin, with its handwoven products and bracelets for sale, lies 13km north of Surin. Afterwards, visit the village of Taklang, home to the Suay people, where small numbers of elephants are trained throughout the year.
Location: Taklang lies 58km north of Surin near the town of Ban Nong Tat.

UDON THANI
From the airbase at Udon Thani the US airforce once dropped bombs on the North Vietnamese and the city still has some decayed nightclubs in its ramshackle streets. Visitors now come here to see Ban Chiang, the nearby village which is the site of one of the oldest civilisations in the world.

Udon Thani has reasonable hotels and is connected to Bangkok by regular trains from Hualomphong Station taking 9 hours and buses which depart from opposite the tourist office.
Location: 564km northeast of Bangkok.

Ban Chiang
If the evidence is to be believed, the

... and imitation, from Ban Chiang

small town of Ban Chiang may well have existed some 5,000 years ago. That evidence comes from pots and stones, green beads and copper bells discovered by villagers during the early part of the century and later by excavations undertaken by the University of Pennsylvania and the Fine Arts Department of Thailand government.

Even more astounding, these pots carry the same thumb-impressed pattern that has been discovered as far afield as Iraq and Turkey.

Besides a delightful museum, with labels in English (open Wednesday to Sunday; admission charge), the small village has open excavation pits containing pots and skulls.
Location: Ban Chiang is situated 50km east of Udon Thani and is reached by the regular bus services.

The Eastern Gulf

PATTAYA

Most people have heard of Pattaya, the sun, sand and sin city. To some it is the closest Thailand gets to paradise; to others it is a seedy, red-light district on the beach. One thing that no-one can possibly deny is that there is no other place like it.

Pattaya's bars are what most people come for rather than its beach, which is brown and grubby. Pubs, beer gardens, boxing rings and cocktail lounges dot the resort where Westerners drink with their Thai girl friends or boy friends. On all sides there are crowded boats, hamburger stalls, revving motorbikes and murky waters.

In all, Pattaya now has more than 21,000 hotel rooms with hundreds more coming on stream. The town is surrounded by massive new condominiums and housing developments. Not content with swimming and partying, the town has introduced waterparks, elephants, golf and even bungee jumping. So don't come here unless you are totally committed to a certain kind of relaxation.

A touch of 'R and R'

King Taksin never knew it, but he may well have been the first man to recognise Pattaya when he camped his army here some 200 years ago. A few fishermen followed his regal example. But for the Americans and the Vietnam war, the place they call 'Westerly Winds' might have stayed little more than a stretch of uninhabited sand and palms.

It did not. When the American soldiers left, the Thais decided that the 'rest and recreation' concept was not such a bad idea and after that the foreign tourists began to like it. Guest houses sprouted up next to hotels and convention centres and condominiums next to bars and brothels. The only thing that did not come into the picture was planning, and Pattaya has paid the price. Many hotels are now suffering water shortages, many of the beaches are short on clean sand and the whole resort suffers a shortage of guests.

That is not to say that people still do not love Pattaya. Many have been coming here year after year and swear they will continue. Many others enjoy the watersports at Jomtien and the islands or merely the feel of a place as Western as it is unreal, where pancakes and waffles are more popular than Thai curries and where dreams, at a price, come true.

Another snap for the tourists

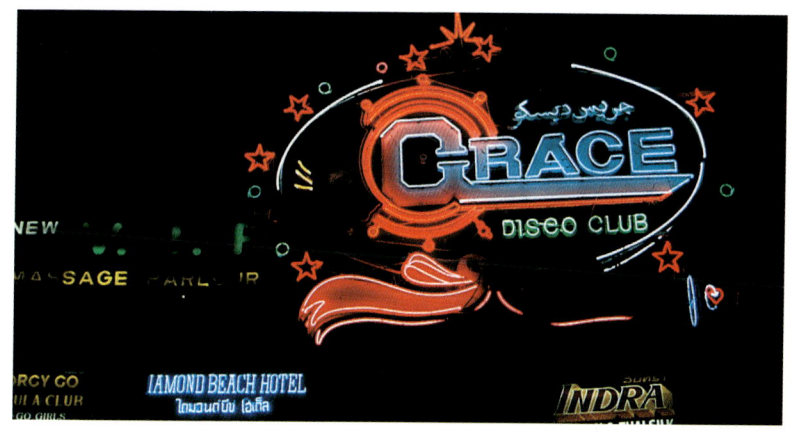

The neon sign trade thrives in Pattaya

Fine hotels, golf courses and good food complete the picture with deep-sea fishing, tennis courts and even a temple on the hill above the town, working overtime to preserve the spirits of those below.

When the lights go out

Pattaya's nightlife has something for every taste, in theory at least. While topless bars and massage parlours predominate, many hotels have respectable piano bars, violinists or cultural shows.

Here you can feast on delicious seafoods fresh from the Gulf of Thailand or any other imaginable Western speciality. But one thing you cannot ignore is the real nightlife. Go-go bars, massage parlours and clubs are Pattaya's blood, its energy. They are to be found all around the town, but especially at the southern end around the area known as Soi Diamond.

Famous shows are another speciality. Even so, caution is essential. The bevy of beautiful girls that you see in the Alcazar Club on Pattaya Road II or the Tiffany Club at the Pattaya Sport Bazaar Building may not be all they seem. Along with hundreds of others in the resort, they are part of Pattaya's considerable population of transvestites. Whilst these clubs have become internationally renowned, other *ka toey (*transvestites*)* hanging out in the bars may be less keen to advertise themselves.

Indeed, for as many men or women who leave Pattaya happy, there are always others who leave walletless or, worse still, carrying the AIDS virus, and while Pattaya may seem a dream, reality can have a nasty knack of catching up.

Getting there

Pattaya is the centre for the so-called 'Thai Riviera'. Nearby towns to the north are Si Racha 28km, Bang Saen 40km and Chon Buri 56km, while Sattahip lies 29km to the south.

Pattaya lies 147km southeast of Bangkok. The town is easily reached by buses that leave every 30 minutes, and take less than 3 hours, from the Eastern Bus Terminal on Sukhumwit Road opposite Soi 42.

The beaches stretch for miles; this is Jomtien

PATTAYA ENVIRONS

Pattaya was designed with day trips in mind. Nearby sights cover the full range from golf courses to tourist villages and from elephants to racing cars, and even a few places to swim.

Motorbikes and jeeps can be hired on a daily basis, while buses and tours cover all the surrounding destinations.

Coral Islands
Pattaya's great lure was once its islands. Many are now expensive and the water not as clear, but they continue to attract vast crowds of local and foreign visitors. The biggest, and still the most popular, is Ko Lan, 45 minutes away by converted trawler, half that time by speed-boat. You can explore the waters around the island (although these are now somewhat polluted) and eat in delicious, if expensive, restaurants.

Alternatively, charter a boat to Ko Phai. It is just 6km further than Ko Lan, has good food and the trip may be just the thing for clearing a heavy head and a full stomach.

Boats can be rented from near the tourist office on Beach Road. Rates vary, so bargain hard.

Elephant Village
This is a popular form of entertainment for children and grown-ups. Elephants demonstrate their strength, skill and obedience before taking a bath in a creek.

Afterwards you can enjoy elephant rides or play with a cheeky baby elephant. Remember to bring a camera.
Location: off Highway 3 at Km144.5. Shows daily. Admission charge.

Jomtien Beach
Once considered a separate resort, Jomtien Beach has gradually become an extension of Pattaya. That has brought the crowds and concrete, but it has managed to survive with less pollution. Jomtien is where most of the windsurfing, sailing and watersports facilities are to be found, as well as some of the best deep-sea fishing in the area.

Nong Nooch, popular with children ...

Even absolute beginners on a day trip often bring in fine catches of marlin and even barracuda, especially between the months of November and February.

Jomtien has fewer bars than Pattaya, fewer restaurants and, for the most part, less of a feel of fun.

Buses and minibuses run regularly between the two resorts which are separated by 6km of headland.

Khao Khieo Open Zoo

The open zoo at Khao Khieo is no African safari park, but it does offer the chance to see some of the wildlife for which Thailand was once renowned. The zoo has Asian, African and European mammals as well as Thailand's most spectacular aviary, the largest in Asia after Singapore. Several walks and trips can be made to forests and waterfalls and there is an education centre and museum. Admission charge.
Location: 34km north of Pattaya, near Bang Saen, and can be reached by local bus.

Nong Nooch Village

The beautifully presented Nong Nooch village resort was designed with the jaded tourist in mind. Orchid nurseries, cactus gardens, landscaped gardens and arts and crafts centres all paint an idyllic picture of the land of smiles. It is all a bit commercialised but, if you have children or will not be able to see the real thing, it can make a pleasant day's outing. Shows start at 10am and 3pm and include folk dances, martial arts, cockfighting and an elephant show.
Location: 18km south of Pattaya. Tours can be arranged through the resort office (tel: 429 321).
Accommodation is also available.

Pattaya Park

This is the closest many people get to water the entire time they are in Pattaya. There are water slides and whirlpools for the children and there is a beer garden, bar and restaurant for the adults. To escape the crowds get there early and avoid weekends.
Location: at 345 Jomtien Beach (tel: 423 000).

... and adults, for both its 'wildlife' and natural history

Beach market, Bang Saen

ANG SILA

Best known as the prolific producer of pestles and mortars, the small fishing town of Ang Sila also has a pleasant bay where fishing boats come in. After Pattaya it is a different world. Fishermen fish and workers work, restaurants sell Thai food and even the bars are just ordinary places for drinking.

If you continue along the coast you will get to a much-vaunted shrine. This marks the spot where Muk, a young Chinese lady, leapt into the sea when her lover married another woman. He was so distraught when he heard the news that he followed suit. Today the shrine is a popular gathering point for locals who make offerings to the amorous duo.
Location: 45km north of Pattaya and 5km from Chon Buri.

BANG SAEN

Nobody ever tried to make Bang Saen a hit with foreigners. Thais had already claimed the closest beach to the capital as their own and every weekend descend in crowds to sit on deckchairs, paddle on dirty sand and eat seafood delicacies. There is a vast aquarium in the Scientific Marine Centre on the university campus, a large waterpark called Ocean World signposted along the seafront, and a long, slightly grubby stretch of sand backed by palm trees from where to watch the world.
Location: 40km from Pattaya. It can also be reached by local buses from Chon Buri

CHANTHA BURI

The gem miners may have been the first to discover Chantha Buri, but the relative charms of the old town and the cool mountain air are slowly beginning to attract growing numbers of tourists. The town is surrounded by lush green hills and, further off, by the fruit fields that have given this area the reputation for being the fruit garden of Thailand.

Getting there

Chantha Buri lies 312km southeast of Bangkok and can be reached by air-conditioned buses leaving the Eastern Bus Terminal in Sukhumvit Road eight times a day. Regular buses and day tours can be organised in Pattaya.

Our Lady Cathedral

The delightful 19th-century Cathedral of the Immaculate Conception is built in the French style. It is frequented by the local Vietnamese and is the largest Catholic cathedral in Thailand.
Location: on the far bank of the Chan Buri river, opposite the Sri Chan Road market.

Gems

These days gems are the main reason for the steady stream of visitors to Chantha Buri. Red rubies and star sapphires are sold in small shops beside the market and along Trok Kachang Road. Inside these dimly lit shops, or sometimes outside in plain daylight, gems are weighed, costed and sold in lots to be exported (or smuggled) around the world.

Some of the gems still come from the mines around Khao Ploi Waan ('Gem mountain'). Growing numbers are, however, imported since most of the local mines have now been exhausted.

Khao Ploi Waan lies 8km north of the town and can be visited on a half-day tour.

Other attractions

Chantha Buri has plenty of other attractions within its armoury: Khao Kitchakut National Park is 28km northeast of town and is renowned for its Krathing waterfall, whilst Khao Sabap National Park is 14km to the southeast and contains the beautiful Phliu Falls.

CHON BURI

The nearest major town to Bangkok, Chon Buri is a major centre for sugar and tapioca. It has a couple of temples, the most famous being Wat Yai Intharam, in the centre of town, dedicated to the famous King Taksin who spent the night there before returning to Ayutthaya to defeat the Burmese. Chon Buri is also the place where buffalo races are celebrated every year in October. Traditionally the buffaloes were helped on their way by a blessing from a Buddhist monk and even a drop of alcohol. With increasing professionalism and bigger rewards, it is now only the owners who get the liquid fortification.

Location: 96km from Bangkok and is reached by regular bus from the Eastern Terminal in Sukhumvit Road.

Pleasing stone carvings, Ang Sila

The white powdery sand of Ko Samet

KO CHANG

The latest paradise islands to draw the attention of developers will not be long in joining Ko Samui and Phuket as prime tourist destinations.

Ko Chang, and the 51 surrounding islands, are scattered around the turquoise waters at the southeastern end of the Gulf, far enough away to be slightly off the main track, but accessible enough by means of a four- or five-day outing.

Ko Chang is the main island. Beyond this lie Ko Kradat, Ko Mak and numerous smaller islands, some of which are still untouched while others are beginning to arouse the interest of tourists.

A few resorts and bungalows already dot the long stretches of white sand on Ko Chang. Inland much of the island is covered with jungle, hosting wildlife and waterfalls.

Location: Laem Ngop, the departure point for Ko Chang, lies 80km from Chantha Buri. To get there catch a bus to Trat and from there a songthaew (truck taxi) to Laem Ngop. One or two boats leave for the main islands daily. The best beaches are on the west side of the island. All visitors are strongly advised to take precautions against malaria which is a major problem.

KO SAMET

Everyone's most popular weekend choice away from Bangkok, Ko Samet is also one of Thailand's most beautiful island national parks and a rapidly developing attraction for the whole province.

It lies just a short distance from the mainland, but far enough away to feel like an island, surrounded by turquoise seas and fringed with palm trees. Indeed, one of Ko Samet's biggest commodities is the pure white crystal sand which covers its beaches. Some of that is enjoyed by appreciative sunbathers, but much of it is of such high quality that it is used by local companies to make glass.

Most visitors come for the sea and sand and place little value on luxurious living. Older and wealthier tourists tend to go to Phuket or Ko Samui where they can indulge in better food and more stylish accommodation. Ko Samet's visitors mainly lie around on the sand, play football on the beaches, listen to guitars and Thai rock music and eat vast amounts of spicy food.

So popular is Ko Samet that getting accommodation at weekends can be almost impossible. Only during the week can you be more of a Robinson Crusoe, although these days you must put up

Fishing is the mainstay of Rayong

> **NAM PLA**
>
> It is smelly and yet the most common accompaniment to Thai food. *Nam pla* is made in Rayong from fermented fish, salt and garlic. You do not have to come all the way here to try it though. Go to any restaurant, ask for *nam pla* and order yourself a large glass of water. If you can get over the initial taste, such is the attraction of the stuff that you may find yourself transporting vast quantities of it home.

with the mounds of rubbish that weekenders inevitably leave behind.
Location: Ko Samet lies 6km off the coast from Ban Phe, to which it is connected by boat. Buses to Ban Phe leave regularly from Bangkok's Eastern Bus Terminal opposite Sukhumvit Soi 42. If you miss the last boat, there are always places to stay in Ban Phe.

RAYONG

Famous for its fishing boats, its *nam pla* (fermented fish) and its rubber plantations, Rayong is not somewhere to spend much time, but the town can make a pleasant stop on the way down the coast. Worth visiting is the King Taksin shrine at Wat Lum Mahachai Chumphon, which commemorates the early Siamese king. You may also come across the statue of Rayong's most famous inhabitant, the man they call Sunthorn Phu, one of the greatest poets Thailand has ever produced, though his work has yet to be translated into English.
Location: Rayong is situated 102km southeast of Pattaya. Regular buses run from Bangkok's Eastern Bus Terminal on Sukhumvit Road.

Southern Thailand

PHUKET

Thailand's most famous beach resort lies off the west coast surrounded by the waters of the Andaman Sea. It is little surprise that it is known as the 'Pearl of the South'.

Phuket (pronounced 'Pooket'), boasts more than 40km of beaches, numerous offshore islands and even a national park. Over the last few years it has also become a haven for the international jet set with its own airport that receives direct flights from Hong Kong, Singapore and Penang, with five-star hotels, nightclubs, restaurants and golf courses.

Some old-timers now complain that it is too expensive and too fashionable. While prices certainly have gone up, and while much of the backpack element has gone, you certainly do not have to be rich or famous to enjoy Phuket. Variety in the choice of resorts, hotels and bungalows means that there is something to cater for every taste, whether you want a berth in an international yacht marina or a simple thatched cottage.

Indeed, while Phuket is no longer the private secret of a few, the simple joys of the sea, the sun and the offshore islands remain just as pervasive as they ever were. It is just that they now come with a touch of the exotic, a touch of the commercial and even a touch of the Western.

Local character

'I know of no place with so much potential' wrote Captain Francis Light, the first man to recognise the riches of Phuket in the early 1770s. Light was referring to the value of the island's vast reserves of tin and he spared little thought for its other commodities of sea and sand. Since then, however, the world has discovered Phuket, and Phuket the world.

Phuket may no longer be the desert hideaway of yesteryear, but it still has something of its own character, as anyone who has seen the Vegetarian Festival will testify. The festival takes

Phuket is set in the Andaman Sea, ideal for all watersports

place during the first nine days of the ninth lunar month (usually mid-September) when many of the local Chinese, having abstained from meat, stick pins through their cheeks and spokes through the skin of their knees. Entranced, they mumble and dance on red-hot coals, and in doing so they purify themselves, an age-old Chinese belief that remains as pervasive today as ever.

At other times of year the locals prefer a less demanding life, going fishing, acting as tour guides or, like the visitors, simply enjoying the balmy evenings and the abundant supplies of lobster, shellfish and prawns served up in bars and restaurants around the island.

Another thing that both locals and foreigners appreciate is some of the most varied terrain and some of the finest seas, not just in Thailand, but anywhere in the world.

Highlights

One feature that distinguishes Phuket, above all others, is its size. Phuket covers an area of 540sq km, almost as large as Corfu. While, geographically, it is an island, the proximity of the mainland (just 100 metres away and connected by bridge) means that there is never a shortage of things to do.

When you have had enough of sun and sea, there is always the Khao Phra Thaeo Wildlife Park, 21km north of Phuket, or the grassy promontory of Prom Thep Cape from which to watch spectacular sunsets over the Andaman Sea.

Another spot not to miss is the beautiful Phuket Aquarium, with over 100 varieties of fish on display. This is situated 10km from Phuket town on the tip of Panwa Cape.

Perhaps the greatest highlight, though, is to hire a motorbike or jeep to explore the island (see page 40). Minibuses also serve the different resorts so that those who do not want to risk driving themselves on the steep winding roads can still move freely around.

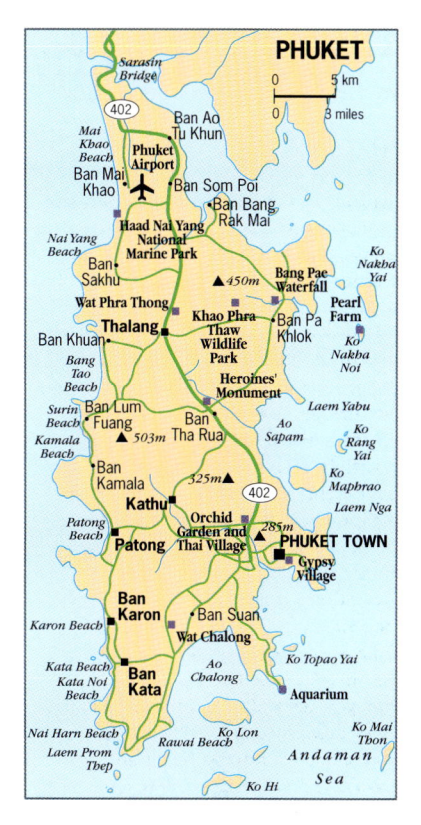

Getting there

Thai International operates direct flights to Phuket from Hong Kong, Singapore and Penang as well as daily flights from Bangkok. These should be booked well in advance. Buses also run from Bangkok's Southern Bus Terminal on Phra Pinklao Road taking around 13 hours.

Phuket Beaches

*I*t is not without good reason that travellers come half-way round the world to visit Phuket: the chief reason they do so is that the island offers some of the world's finest beaches.

These are mainly located down the sandy, palm-lined west coast, separated by coves and hills. Forget the east coast; it is fringed with mangroves. Each beach has something of its own character and each offers a variety of accommodation and leisure activities.

Most visitors, once they have settled in, rarely move. The temptations of sun and sea are too much. So, like choosing a holiday, it pays to shop around and to opt for something that will suit both your pocket and your disposition. The choice is enormous.

The curving stretch of Karon Beach

Patong

Rising up from the western coast, the sprinkling of bungalows rapidly gives way to towers, shopping arcades, rows of beer bars, hotels and discos. Big, loud and international, Patong has rapidly overtaken the other resorts to become the king of nightlife and of glitzy entertainment. That does not, however, overshadow its other qualities. Patong also has some of the best and whitest beaches with non-stop watersports: parasailing, jet skis, speed-boats and windsurfing. One thing Patong is not renowned for is quiet, so if that is what you are after, somewhere further down the coast may prove a safer bet.

Location: 15km west of Phuket town.

Karon/Kata

Quiet, calm and exclusive, the long curving stretch of Karon Beach, situated half-way down the western coast, has rapidly developed into an up-market, but largely family-oriented, area with a string of five-star hotels with swimming pools and garden terraces. Inland there are still plenty of bars, restaurants and discos, but they are less imposing and less noisy than those of Patong. Just around the headland is Kata, a smaller stretch of beautiful white sand divided into two parts. Kata hosts a number of smart hotels and restaurants, but also many cheaper establishments and bars.
Location: 16km southwest of Phuket town.

Para-gliding is the latest craze to hit Phuket

Surin/Pansea

The connoisseur's choice, away from the hustle and bustle. People who come to Surin/Pansea almost inevitably stay in one of the exclusive hotels hidden by palm trees and coconuts yet overlooking the shores. Do not expect lines of nightclubs though. Surin may have come a long way in the last few years, but it still remains pretty much in its own world, largely cut off from the other beaches by poor roads and still a fair distance from Phuket town. The quality of swimming in Surin does not, however, rank with the other resorts and currents can be dangerous.
Location: 24km northwest of Phuket town.

Smaller beaches

To the north of Patong are the smaller and quieter beaches of **Kamala Bay** and **Laem Sing**. A few exclusive hotels dot the area and development is firmly under way. So far, however, this stretch of land offers the closest to Phuket as it was in the old days, with children playing undisturbed on the beaches and just the odd speed-boat breaking the silence. Beware conditions, however. During the monsoon season, the weather creates vicious undercurrents and can make swimming unsafe. Always check with the locals before you go into the water as it can be deceptive.

Uncrowded hideaways

Once hideaways were everywhere; now they are a dying breed. But there are some quieter spots around the island, generally not far from the big resorts. For real calm try the secluded half-moon beach of **Nai Yang**, to the northwest, which has been set aside as a national park and where, at low tide, you can walk for long distances along a relatively deserted coastline.

Uncrowded too is the long stretch of **Mai Khao Beach** that lies further north and where, between October and February, giant sea turtles come to lay their eggs and where palms give way to pine trees and picnic spots.

PHUKET ENVIRONS

Phuket's beaches may be its main attractions, but there is no shortage of sights which can be easily reached as part of a day trip. Almost every big hotel will organise tours. Alternatively go to any of the local travel agents.

NAKHA NOI PEARL FARM

Nakha Noi Pearl Farm is one of the world's largest and best-known cultured-pearl farms. Like others in the vicinity, Nakha Noi is run by Japanese who seed oysters to produce the dazzling small stones that are exported to markets around the world.

A few years ago the farm managed to produce the world's largest cultured pearl, a monster 40mm in diameter and weighing just over 30g. These days you may not come across pearls of that size, but at Nakha Noi Farm, and at several other farms within the province, you can still see how they are cultured.

Location: Nakha Noi Pearl Farm is situated on an island off the eastern coast in Po Bay, 22km north of Phuket town. Shows are at 11am daily. Admission charge. Contact Nakha Pearl Tour and Resort (tel: 219 870).

The extraordinary Ko Tapu (Nail Island), off Phang Nga

Ko Panyi, the sea gypsy village

PHANG NGA

But for the James Bond film *The Man with the Golden Gun*, Phuket's top tourist destination might have remained comparatively unknown. Ever since they were featured in the film, the weird and wonderful limestone formations that rise up sheer out of the sea have succeeded in captivating the world and ushering in thousands of tourists every day.

Many lie far out to sea where they house secret caves and can only be reached by using special inflatable rafts.

Daily tours will, however, take you by boat to see Ko Tapu (Nail Island) with its impossibly sheer rock face climbing out from the water. Most trips also include a trip to the fishing village of Ko Panyi, a small Muslim community on stilts which is rapidly swapping fishing for tourism, where a seafood lunch of prawns and lobster is likely to prove the treat of the day. En route you will be shown a cliff known as Khao Khian (Old Writing) covered in paintings which date back thousands of years and which may be some of the earliest of Thailand's prehistoric remains.

At one point you must pass through a rock tunnel, a favourite spot for photographers who try to frame the picture with a small fishing boat passing through. At other times you will catch views of enchanting outcrops dotted around the sea.

For the more adventurous, dinghy trips can be arranged to view cave interiors or to travel to the more distant islands where the magic of Phang Nga remains as yet largely unexplored.
Location: Phang Nga is 90km to the northeast of Phuket. Regular buses leave the Phuket Bus Terminal taking 2 hours. Most people opt for full-day tours.

SIMILAN ISLANDS

The nine Similan Islands are renowned among diving enthusiasts. They offer some of the most spectacular underwater sightseeing in the Andaman Sea. Wisely the authorities have seen fit to turn the area into a national park where nature remains relatively at peace and where the corals and colourful marine life are left more or less intact. It is best to come during the months of December to May when the waters are at their clearest and the skies are normally a cloudless blue. Part of the islands' appeal lies in their relative solitude. Rarely do the beaches bear the scars of the new invaders, mostly day trippers who are gone by the time night falls. For those staying longer, bungalows and camping are available on Ko Similan. Boats can be hired to the other main islands of Ko Ba Ngu and Ko Miang and, these days, often to Ko Born, Ko Payu and Ko Payang.
Location: the Similans lie off the western coast of Thailand and can be reached from Phuket in 8 hours by regular boat or in 3½ hours as part of Songserm Travel's fast day trip. Contact Songserm at 64/2 Rassada Shopping Centre, Phuket town (tel: 222 570). Between July and November the islands may be inaccessible because of the monsoon.

SOUTHERN THAILAND

HAT YAI

Hat Yai, southern Thailand's largest city, has not grown to what it is as the result of history nor, for that matter, for its beauty, but because of two equally marketable commodities: with its proximity to Malaysia (50km away) and its *laissez-faire* attitude, it has become the entertainment centre for Malaysian men and a booming centre for smuggled goods.

As a consequence, it has also become the fastest-growing city in the south, far outpacing neighbouring Songkhla, to become a sex and sin metropolis *par excellence*. Down almost every street you will come across a palatial-looking massage parlour or bars where girls dressed in purple skirts and high-heeled shoes sing love songs until the early hours of the morning.

For non-Malay visitors, Hat Yai has also made an effort to provide entertainment of a different kind, notably shopping, restaurants and markets.

Getting there

Hat Yai is situated 933km south of Bangok. Trains leave Bangkok's Hualamphong station several times daily taking 19 hours. Buses leave from the Southern Bus Terminal on Phra Pinklao Road. Thai Airways International also has daily flights.

Bullfighting

On the first Saturday of the month Hat Yai hosts another celebrated spectacle, the bullfight. Do not expect matadors and red cloaks though. Bullfights here are of a less dramatic quality than in Spain. The bulls fight each other rather than facing a human combatant. Two beasts are brought face to face and left to their own devices. Often the bulls do not move for hours on end, giving time for new bets to be placed. Then all of a sudden, one lowers its head and charges, or the two animals lock horns and push against each other. A victor is declared if one bull runs away or gives ground.
Location: the bullfighting is held at the Klong Wa stadium near the city bus terminal off Rajyindee Road.

Shopping

Hat Yai's best shopping is to be found off Niphat Uthit 2 and 3 Roads where you will find cheap electronic goods smuggled over the border, fake designer T-shirts and handbags. For something different, try the vendors around the Mitrama Hotel on Channiwet Road. They sell the hottest cocktail in town: snake's blood mixed with alcohol.

Another Hat Yai speciality to look out for are doves kept in beautifully carved cages. The birds are used for local cooing contests with considerable amounts of money awarded to the winners.

Songkhla

A gentle 30-minute bus ride from the busy streets of Hat Yai brings you to Songkhla, the older, more respectable

Painted fishing boat, Songkhla

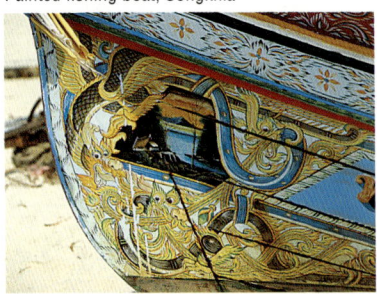

Hat Yai and neighbouring Songkhla lie south of Bangkok, near the Malaysian border. Nearby sights are the bird sanctuary of Thale Noi at Phattalung, 90km north, and the Khu Khut Waterbird Sanctuary, 40km northeast, near the town of Sathing Phra.

and calmer sister. Songkhla has history and beaches, a delightful fishing port and the air of a long-forgotten place. You do not see masseuses and coachloads of Malaysians, but you do see people coming to enjoy fresh seafood, piles of prawns and picnics on the sand.

Getting there
Buses run from Hat Yai to Songkhla every 30 minutes until early evening.

Beaches
Beaches may not be Songkhla's main attraction, but they remain popular with the locals. Samila stretches for some 5km along a fairly ordinary stretch of water backed by casuarina trees. Crowds are never a problem, but the sea can be rough.
Location: Samila Beach lies 3km northeast of the town centre. Offshore are the rocky islands known as the 'Cat and Mouse'.

Fast-growing Hat Yai contains a vast number of different shops

National Museum
Songkhla's former Governor's Palace is a museum piece in its own right. The 1870s building, a delightful example of Sino-Portuguese architecture, houses a good collection of Srivijayan art as well as items belonging to former governors.
Location: off Vichianchom Road. Open: from Wednesday to Sunday, 9am–4pm. Admission charge.

Other attractions
You can climb up **Mount Tangkuan**, with its *chedis* (pagodas) and its fine views of the inland sea, or visit the charming old Sino-Portuguese shop-houses on **Nakhon Nok** and **Nakhon Nai Streets**. Songkhla will never set the world alight, but it will set the soul at peace.

HUA HIN

A quarter of the way down the coast, on the way to the more exotic destinations of Ko Samui and Phuket, is the seaside resort of Hua Hin, known as the 'Royal Resort'.

Prince Chakrabongsae and King Rama VII were two of its earliest admirers. They came here to escape the heat of the capital and prompted the Siamese gentry to follow suit. These days, however, you are more likely to run into modern concrete hotels and condominiums than palaces and aristocracy.

Still, if you are not expecting palm trees and palaces, Hua Hin still exerts its charms, with its beach which was made to potter on (rather than for bathing), the blue and red deckchairs made for sitting on and the cluster of old ladies offering traditional massage.

For a glimpse of the old way of life, wander down towards the pier, which is reached by walking through the old part of town. Take a seat in one of the waterfront restaurants along Naretdamn Road and enjoy some of the wonderful seafood. Nobody will take much notice of you. Only at weekends is the beach crowded with locals escaping from Bangkok.

In the evening Hua Hin sheds some of its respectability; then the beer bars and outdoor markets come alive, but never to the extent of Pattaya, the sex and sin centre which nestles almost directly opposite on the Gulf of Thailand.

Getting there

Buses leave approximately every 30 minutes from Bangkok's Southern Bus Terminal on Phra Pinklao Road. By far the most pleasant way of arriving is by train from Bangkok's Hualamphong station, which takes four hours. The train stops at the little gem of a station which is itself a monument to Hua Hin's past. Bangkok Airways also offers daily flights from Bangkok's domestic airport.

A strange temple at Hua Hin, known as Wat Khao Ta Kiab

WHAT TO SEE

Hua Hin lies 220km south of Bangkok. Nearby sights are Cha-am, 25km north, the historic town of Phetcha Buri, 66km north and the beaches of Prachup Khiri Khan, 90km south.

Despite the multi-storey, Hua Hin is still a fairly old-fashioned resort

Cha-am

Hua Hin's little sister was, until a few years ago, largely eclipsed. These days the locals have taken a liking to it, although foreigners still prefer the older sister's charm.

Cha-am's sandy beach is long and wide and offers the delights of seafood and paddling. Around the back you will find a small fishing port where you can sit on the rocks and watch the fishing boats steaming out to sea.

There is no need to stay here, though. Hotels in Hua Hin are better. Even so, for a short trip on the regular bus, it makes a nice break and a good way to see something of the countryside.
Location: 25km to the north of Hua Hin.

Chopstick Hill

At the southern end of Hua Hin beach is the huge Buddha of Chopstick Hill. If you continue 8km further south, you will reach the protected bay of Khao Tao, once very peaceful but now being developed.
Location: 6km south of Hua Hin.
Songthaews *(truck taxis) run regularly.*

Sam Roi Yod

For a pleasant afternoon's trip, visit the lovely Sam Roi Yod National Park, famed among ornithologists for its marsh birds and waders. King Rama IV came here in 1868 to witness an eclipse of the sun, although he died of malaria shortly afterwards. Around the park are beautiful caves, and boats can be hired.
Location: 35km south of Hua Hin. To reach it you will need private transport or you can join a tour.

THE OLD RAILWAY HOTEL

No other establishment, save perhaps for the royal residence of Klai Kangwon ('Far from Worries') has become such a hallmark of Hua Hin as the building known until recently as the Old Railway Hotel. For years this was the preserve of the gentry and, during the 1970s, it served as the location for the film the *Killing Fields*. Under the management of the French Sofitel group, the hotel still remains the pre-eminent hotel in Hua Hin.

ROYALTY

Queen Sirikit

King Bhumipol Adulyadej Chakri of Thailand

Royal barges, Bangkok

Bhumipol Adulyadej Chakri: the name is carved in gold on the hearts of his subjects, written with pride. No single figure contributes so much to the well-being of the people as the King of Thailand, ninth in the line of the Chakri dynasty.

Born on 5 December 1927, he was made king upon the untimely death of his brother and, over the last 45 years, has become the most beloved and the most respected of the Chakri monarchs.

Seen dressed in finery, or carried downriver on a royal barge, he is the very essence of royalty, the veritable Siamese monarch of old. For most of the year, however, the king is away from the public eye, inspecting new agricultural methods in the provinces or pioneering irrigation schemes in the interest of his subjects.

When disaster strikes, the king leaves his palace, flying or trekking into the furthest reaches of the kingdom to offer consolation. In times of uncertainty, the king is looked upon as saviour, as judge or as the guardian of the people.

Every December he takes the salute of the nation on the occasion of his birthday. Every day, at 6pm, the national anthem is played on radios and in parks around the country. Even in the homes of his subjects, he is rarely forgotten. Pictures of the king and the royal family hang in almost every house, the pride of every heart. Thailand has no other.

Birthday celebrations for the King, Chiang Rai

KO SAMUI

The word *Ko* means island and Samui must be the archetypal one at that. The two words have become well known among beach lovers around the world. Once, though, it was only the backpackers who knew them. Now Ko Samui is increasingly prized among up-market tourists who fly in for weekends from Bangkok or further afield, landing on the island's small airstrip.

Gone are the many signs advertising magic mushrooms and the sense of a small community on the edge of a breakthrough. Many former plot owners are now millionaires while others are involved with the development of bars and discothèques.

It takes a monkey four to five days to learn to spin a coconut off its stem

Even so, Ko Samui has preserved the feel of a tropical island, with its palms and white sandy beaches. Here you can still sit in peace and solitude to watch the sunset from the balcony of a simple bungalow. Even the spattering of new four- and five-star developments, the growing nightlife, the discos and restaurants have failed to wrest that away.

Coconut territory

If Phuket's coastline is broken up by coves and bays, Ko Samui has one continuous beach running for almost its entire length, while the inland coconut palms have made it one of the biggest exporters of coconuts in Thailand.

That suits every taste, for while Phuket is about activity, watersports and entertainment, Ko Samui is about relaxation, and only the motorbikes and the tarmac strip around the island hint at the growing inroads of the modern world.

Most visitors explore no further than the Hin Lat waterfall, signposted 2km south of Na Thon, or the strange 'Grandfather' rock formations at the end of Lamai Beach.

Others catch glimpses of the famous pig-tailed macaque monkeys, fervent workers who have put men out of jobs since they are trained to pick up to 1,000 coconuts a day. Otherwise you will not find much to do, save to eat a seafood (or Western) lunch, sunbathe in a hammock, or take a windsurfing board on the water.

Occasionally even Ko Samui bursts into life when there is a bullfight, but these do not last long and soon the inhabitants drift back to their coconuts and the foreigners to their sand, their videos, restaurants and discos.

WHAT TO SEE

Ko Samui lies 80km off shore from Suratthani. Nearby mainland sights are the historical towns of Nakhon Si Thammarat, 134km to the south, and Chaiya, 40km due west.

Ko Samui: clear blue sea and white sand

Beaches
Everyone on Ko Samui has a favourite beach, though the speed with which things have developed means that the choice is increasingly segmented into different price ranges.

Chaweng is still the most popular. The main strip, and home to many of the smart hotels, lies on the east coast, reached by a long climbing road. The smart developments lie at one end, set among palm trees and exotic gardens, but there is still plenty for those with humbler requirements.

Lamai is a curving bay further to the south. Smaller, humbler, broken up by rocks and coves, it is still more for the backpackers, although new hotels are making their appearance. Hundreds of huts dot the seafront, but the curving beach breaks up any sense of overcrowding. For the evening, several discos and restaurants have sprung up behind the beach.

Choeng Mon, less well known and more exclusive, is set along a beautiful small bay at the northern tip of the island. It is home to several large hotels and to a beach lined with coconut palms and casuarina trees.

Big Buddha Beach, further round to the west, is less popular, but has fine views of two offshore islands. It is beautiful during the summer but choppy during the monsoons, with conditions that may not be suitable for swimming.

All these beaches can be reached by *songthaews* (truck taxis) which circulate from the main town of Na Thon until 6pm. Motorbikes and jeeps can also be hired, although care should be taken.

Getting there
Bangkok Airways flies several times daily from Bangkok to Ko Samui taking just one hour. Alternatively, you can take the daily train from Bangkok's Hualamphong station to Suratthani (see page 125), a journey of 12 hours. From Suratthani a speed-boat leaves three times a day taking two hours to reach Na Thon on Ko Samui. You are advised to buy a combined rail/ferry ticket which includes transfer.

A gold Buddha from Nakhon

AROUND KO SAMUI

Once on Ko Samui, you are assured of variety. The island is surrounded by some 80 smaller islands, of which the best known are Ko Phangan and Ko Tao, as well as the beautiful Ang Thong Marine National Park. These can be seen either as part of an organised tour or by regular boats from Ko Samui.

Ang Thong Marine Park

Names like 'Sleeping Cow Island', 'Tripod Island' and 'Kicking Cow Island', give visitors an idea of what to expect from the Ang Thong Marine Park which lies 29km to the northwest of Ko Samui. For the strange-shaped islands of this archipelago are like gems of rock dropped from the sky and congealed in every shape, size and form.

Beautiful caves and waterfalls can be reached along signposted trails that cut through the scenery of forest and limestone. 'Sleeping Cow Island' (Ko Wua Ta Lap) is the most popular island offering fine views, bungalows and a campsite. Alternatively, try Ko Mae Ko with its crystal-clear saltwater lagoon.

Daily boat trips to Ang Thong Marine Park are organised by most tour agents on Ko Samui, leaving Na Thon at 8.30am and returning at 5pm. For those impressed with what they see, longer stays can be arranged.

Ko Phangan

Ko Phangan, the undeveloped sister island, is just an hour's hop north of Ko Samui by boat, but in terms of scenery and facilities it is like moving to another world.

Rough dirt roads circle the island, a reminder of days gone by on Samui. A better alternative for those wishing to avoid the endless jolting is to take a boat, either to the southeastern tip of Haad Rin or to the northwest coast around Mae Haad Bay.

On the island you will find white beaches dotted with palm trees and small bungalows where the talk among backpackers is of discovering the next beach paradise and where immediate concerns go no further than the next meal. Offshore there are opportunities for snorkelling with several bungalows now offering flippers and a face mask.

Those who appreciate their luxuries can now visit Ko Phangan for the day. Boats leave Bo Phut Beach on Ko Samui in the morning, arriving at Hat Rin 50 minutes later. That gives just about enough time for a swim and a seafood lunch before catching the return boat to Ko Samui in the afternoon. There are plenty of tours.

Ko Tao

Those in search of greater isolation can also visit Ko Tao, the island that lies three hours north of Ko Phangan and where people spend weeks on end living in small bungalows, eating prawns and coconuts and playing at being a modern-day Robinson Crusoe.

Boats leave irregularly to Ko Tao from Thong Sala pier on Ko Phangan.

Suratthani

Suratthani is not one of the great destinations of the south – the mainland jumping-off point for Ko Samui and the islands of Ko Phangan and Ko Tao is more a transit point than a destination in its own right.

A busy market and a host of food stalls do, however, offer consolation if you are waiting for a boat, while several hotels and guest houses provide a resting spot for those who have missed it.

Other attractions

Those of cultural bent may prefer to leave the town and head north for 40km to the historical town of **Chaiya**. If archaeologists are right this may once have been the capital of the Srivijaya Kingdom, one of the oldest and most powerful in Asia.

Others may prefer the town of **Nakhon Si Thammarat**, 134km to the south, with its history and its nearby beaches, valued by the locals as a secret, but increasingly known by foreigners as an escape. Both are reached by bus or train from Suratthani.

Getting there

Trains leave Bangkok's Hualamphong station daily for Suratthani taking 12 hours. VIP also runs air-conditioned coaches to Suratthani from Bangkok.

Wat Mahathat in Nakhon

KRABI

One of the finest gems in Thailand's beach crown is summed up in one word: Krabi – a world of limestone cliffs fringed by long white beaches that lies a couple of hours east of Ko Phi Phi and a 3-hour road (or boat) trip from Phuket.

Ao Nang is the most accessible of Krabi's beaches with continually developing accommodation. It can be reached by a 25-minute boat trip from Krabi pier or a spectacular road trip through the cliffs.

Ao Phranang is reached only by boat from either Krabi pier or Ao Nang Beach, but is far more beautiful, with a curving bay, an offshore island and impressive views from Princess Cave. Accommodation, however, is basic and at high season it can be crowded.

Location: 170km from Phuket by road. Buses leave Phuket two or three times daily from the terminal on Phangnga Road. Songserm Travel also operates buses from Bangkok.

The Phi Phi Islands

The most beautiful islands in the world – so say many of the sun-tanned foreigners who have travelled the world looking for the most idyllic hideaway and finally come across the twin islands known as Ko Phi Phi.

The Phi Phi islands are two gems surrounded by palm trees with dreamy bays, spectacular limestone cliffs and long sandy beaches.

While Phuket has luxury and Ko Samui an international airport, many parts of Phi Phi have yet to get electricity. The islands do get their fair share of tourists, though, and at certain times it can be extremely difficult finding accommodation.

Getting there

Phi Phi Don, the bigger of the two islands and the main arrival point, lies equidistant between Krabi and Phuket. Boats run five times daily from Patong Beach on Phuket taking 2 to 3 hours. Boats run three times daily from Krabi taking around 2 hours. Boat trips run in the monsoon season and are only cancelled if a storm is imminent.

Bird's nest soup

Foreigners were not the first people to

The sea lake on Phi Phi Le is formed by a cleft between two limestone cliffs

The Phi Phi Islands nestle two hours' offshore from mainland Krabi and are within easy reach of Phuket, Ko Lanta and Ko Hai.

recognise Phi Phi's potential. The Chinese got here years ago but, rather than opting for a beach holiday, they found a more lucrative resource: the raw ingredients for bird's nest soup. These tiny swiftlets' nests, made up of bird spittle and long renowned for their revitalising quality, can only be reached by climbing bamboo ladders high up in the mouths of the local caves. It is worth it though, since the nests fetch a very high price in the open market.

You can see where the nests come from by visiting **Viking Cave** on Phi Phi Le. Only at certain times of year are visitors allowed, so as not to disturb the mating swallows. At other times of the year you must content yourself with the island's other attractions – boat trips, lazing under palm trees and eating fresh seafood, lobster and freshly picked coconuts.

Around the islands

Popularity is as yet restricted to the larger

Phra Nang beach – some people's idea of paradise, but Krabi is developing fast

island of Phi Phi Don. The other island, Phi Phi Le, has no accommodation, although a steady stream of visitors takes advantage of the numerous boats that cross over daily to visit **Viking Cave** and the beautiful **Maya Bay.** Here you can snorkel and picnic. Further around the bay there is another chance to explore the underwater corals, then it's back through the turquoise seas to Phi Phi Don in time to watch the sunset.

Experienced divers are spoilt by even greater choice. Underwater coral has made the Phi Phi Islands renowned and, despite damage to the reef caused by the rapid influx of admirers, there is still plenty to see.

Diving trips can be booked, along with deep-sea fishing trips and day tours of the islands, from any of the agents near the pier.

Tarutao: fine beaches as well as a protected wildlife area

TARUTAO

Nearing the end of the long trunk-like isthmus of Thailand, offshore from the town of Ban Pak Bara, lie the 51 islands that make up the Tarutao Marine National Park.

Unknown until recently, the islands remain off the beaten track, still difficult to get to, yet set in beautiful surroundings in the Indian Ocean.

In the 1980s the islands were declared a national park and they are now closely monitored by officials trying to preserve the environment. So far development on the islands has been minimal. Instead you have to put up with dormitories or, if you are lucky, bungalows and tents.

During World War II Tarutao was a penal colony. Now visitors come for the beaches with its famous powdery white sand, the islands' inland waterfalls and caves. Diving is one of the great pleasures and boats can be hired to explore the surroundings.

Tarutao is the largest of the 51 islands in the national park, covering an area of 151sq km, but within reasonable reach are the lesser known sister islands of Adang, Rawi and Lipe.

Getting there

Buses leave fairly regularly from Bangkok's Southern Bus Terminal to Trang (can take several hours). From there you must catch a *songthaew* (truck taxi) to the small fishing village of Ban Pak Bara. Boats to Tarutao leave from here twice daily in season.

PEOPLE OF THE DEEP SOUTH

More than 2 million Muslims live in the provinces that make up the far south of Thailand. They are the biggest minority in the kingdom, a people who have traditionally sided with Malaysia. Most of them are farmers or fishermen living in small communities, although several big towns do exist. In the past friction with the Thais and calls for a separate homeland has marred the situation in the south. These days trouble is rare, but a strong military presence, as well as a royal palace, are there to make sure it stays that way.

TOWNS OF THE DEEP SOUTH

NARATHIWAT

When you get to Narathiwat, you have almost reached the end of the road, as far as Thailand is concerned. Beyond lie the border towns of Sungai Kolok and Ban Taba.

Few visitors come this far south. Anyone who does will discover a town lazily unaware of its own charms, with its wide shady streets crossed by tricycles and its inhabitants dressed in colourful Muslim clothes and batik.

The locals seem in little hurry to change that, the only apparent sign of activity being in the markets.

A 6km *songthaew* (truck taxi) ride to the southwest of the town is the **Wat Khao Kong**, with its vast bronze

Although the majority of the population of the far south are Muslims, wats still abound; this one is in Yala

Wat Tham Ku Ha Phimuk

Buddha, 25m high. At the other end of town is **Hat Narathiwat Beach** and the sea, less developed than elsewhere in the south, and with less exotic appeal, but still good for a paddle (beware the currents) or as a place to eat local snacks.

Location: Narathiwat is 1,315km from Bangkok and can be reached by buses from the Southern Bus Terminal on Phra Pinklao Road.

PATTANI AND YALA

Easily reached northwest from Narathiwat are Pattani, 100km, and Yala, 108km. These towns bear the hallmarks of Islam and something of the influence of nearby Malaysia. Few tourists come down this way; they are told it is unsafe because of separatist conflicts. Visitors should check the local station. Those that do will almost inevitably be rewarded with glimpses of unspoilt rural villages and beautiful countryside.

Both towns are connected to Narathiwat by bus. Yala is also on the main railway line between Hat Yai and Malaysia.

Getting Away From it All

*A*dventure travel in Thailand may have lessened with the opening up of the kingdom and the rapid influx of tourists, but the sheer size of the country and the fact that visitors concentrate on a small handful of sights, means that there is always something different near at hand for those with a little more time or a sense of adventure.

Most trips can be organised using public transport. These days there is also no shortage of travel companies offering tours and the bigger hotels always have something organised.

There are two things to remember: do not go off into isolated areas alone and beware the border areas, especially around the Golden Triangle. Outside of that make the most of the opportunities. Thailand still has some of the most beautiful and undiscovered spots in the East and people who make the effort to find them will almost inevitably be well rewarded.

BIRD WATCHING

Colourful waders, orange-breasted and red-headed trogons, moustached barbets and kingfishers are just some of the birds that can be found in the national parks. They are part of a vast ornithological population which is estimated to include over 900 species of bird. Some are unique to Thailand. Others migrate from as far afield as Northern China and Siberia leaving winter far behind them.

Two of the best spots for the visiting birdwatcher are the **Thale Noi Bird Sanctuary** and the **Khu Khut Waterbird Sanctuary**, both within easy access of Hat Yai and Songkhla (see pages 116–17). Trips can be arranged from either town through tours or by taking public transport. **Khao Yai National Park**, situated just a couple of hours northeast of Bangkok, also has one of the highest concentrations of hornbills in Southeast Asia (see page 69). Another good and more accessible place to go is the **Khao Khieo Open Zoo** near Pattaya (see page 105).

Birds are abundant along Thailand's coast because the marine life of the mudflats is rich and food is plentiful

GETTING AWAY FROM IT ALL

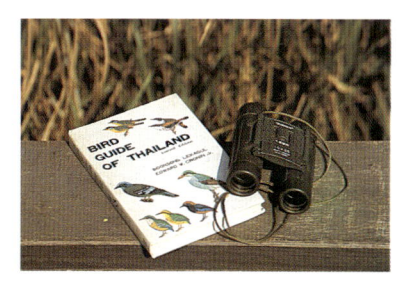

Essential luggage for the twitcher

Remember to bring binoculars, a book for identification and a lot of patience; Thailand may still have many birds, but those that are left have grown wise to the ways of the world and are often heard but rarely seen.

BUDDHIST MEDITATION

It may not be adventure travel in the physical sense, but Buddhist meditation is rapidly being accepted throughout the Western world, with no better place to try it than Thailand itself.

Courses can last for anything from one day to two weeks and range in content from simple meditation to vigorous pursuit of the key precepts. Those who wish to attend meditation classes during their stay in Bangkok can do so at **Wat Mahathat**. Classes are also held at **Wat Bowonniwet** and at the **World Fellowship of Buddhists**.

Outside the capital, one of the most popular centres is located at **Suan Mokhapalaram** in Suratthani Province, where a large, tree-filled park provides an ideal atmosphere for discovering peace of mind. Classes last for 10 days from the first of each month.

CAVING

Until someone produced statistics showing that Thailand has one of the biggest caves in the world, no one really bothered about them much except as a setting for Buddha statues. Now people are beginning to explore them, although a local guide is essential. Probably the best known is **Tham Lot Cave**, situated 9km from the town of Soppong in Mae Hong Son Province (see page 90); further down the road is another vast cave. Guides can be hired at the Cave Lodge Guest House. In the south, caves can be explored on **Ao Phranang** near Krabi (see page 126) and at **Phang Nga** near Phuket (see page 114).

One of the many limestone caves at Phang Nga; mind the bats

Powerful tourist boats bring even the remotest islands within reach

CLIMBING

Thailand's highest peak, Doi Inthanon near Chiang Mai, only reaches 2,565m so there is not much opportunity for alpine sports or ropes and crampons. The country does, however, have plenty of opportunities for steep hiking. **Khao Yai** (see page 69), **Loei** (see page 96) and **Doi Inthanon** (see page 80) all offer slopes sufficiently steep to make even the fittest person pant. Before attempting them contact the National Parks Division in Bangkok *(tel: 579 0529)* for details and enquire about a guide. You are unlikely to find sheer rock faces, but you will find fine views and staggeringly beautiful countryside.

ISLAND HOPPING

You do not have to go far in Thailand to find a perfect island, but to find an uninhabited one or to explore a whole string of them takes more time and trouble.

The best starting off points for island hopping are **Krabi** and **Ko Phi Phi** (see page 126) and **Phuket** (see page 114). The best method of exploring them is either by charter (relatively expensive) or by regular public boat services.

From Ko Phi Phi you can jump on a regular boat which will take you to **Ko Lanta** and from there to **Ko Hai** and **Ko Muk**. Some people have even managed to work their way all the way down to **Ko Tarutao** in the far south. On the east coast, there are regular boats from Chumphon to **Ko Tao** and from there to **Ko Phangan** and **Ko Samui**.

New services are springing up all the time to make access to the many other islands a great deal easier but, conversely, they make the desert island discovery more elusive.

MOTORBIKING

Motorbikes provide one of the best and most popular ways of getting to see the countryside. 125cc, 250cc and even 750cc bikes can now be rented by the day, especially in Chiang Mai, Bangkok and Phuket.

Some of the best motorbiking is to be

found in the winding roads and dirt tracks of the north, around Chiang Mai, Mae Sai and the Golden Triangle.

From here you can tour around Chiang Rai or follow the road circuit westwards via Pai to Mae Hong Son and Mae Sariang. Roads are generally in reasonable condition, although beware oncoming trucks and buses which take up the whole road. Also never, never drive at night or by yourself.

Motorbikes generally cost upwards of bt300 a day, although the big bikes are correspondingly more. All you really need is a 125cc bike but preferably a petrol rather than a diesel guzzler (and make sure you know which before you leave).

Before you go, check the bike as you will be responsible for any damage sustained on the way. Finally beware: accidents and injuries are numerous.

NATIONAL PARKS

National parks, to anyone who has been to Africa, mean abundant wildlife, herds of elephants and the occasional giraffe. Thailands parks offer sights that are different but as good: beautiful nature, flowers and waterfalls and some of the last unspoilt spots in the country.

With as many as 53 national parks scattered throughout the kingdom, there is no lack of choice. Some parks are on the mainland, while others consist of islands. Some are reached by boat, others by jeep or bus.

From Bangkok the most popular and easily accessable is **Khao Yai** (see page 69), which has one of the largest concentrations of wildlife in the country. In the south are the island parks of **Tarutao** (see page 128) and the **Similans** (see page 115). In the north and northeast are **Doi Inthanon** (see page 80) and **Phu Kradung** (see page 97).

Most national parks have accommodation and some even provide meals. If you are planning on spending time there always make a reservation in advance and, if you are thinking of trekking, try to arrange a guide as well as maps, sleeping bags, malaria tablets and a Thai dictionary. For bookings, contact the National Parks Division on Phahon Yothin Road in Bankgok *(tel: 579 0529)*.

One of the easiest, but by no means the safest way to explore Thailand

WILDLIFE

The rich forests, countryside, coasts and hills of Thailand are breeding grounds for some of the last true remaining wildlife in Asia. Elephants, monkeys, tortoises and beautiful birds are all part of Nature's gift to the kingdom, and while man has cut down many of the trees and taken away many of the forest inhabitants, others remain living in the wild.

The most common species still found in Thailand are gibbons, macaque monkeys and sambar deer, although even these are a dwindling force. An estimated 200 tigers are also said to live wild in the Burmese border areas, along with rapidly declining numbers of elephants. The elephant is Thailand's most revered animal and national symbol, once featured on

Two northern locals – gibbon and lotus blossom

Thailand natives: tigers (but you have to be very lucky to spot them)

its flag, but that hasn't deterred the poachers.

In desperation, one chief warden at a national park was driven to commit suicide because his rangers were repeatedly attacked by elephant poachers armed with sophisticated military weapons.

Thailand's forests, flowers and lush tropical vegetation are more easily enjoyed. In the north, especially, there are still large areas of evergreen and teak forest protected under national park status, while the south has vast areas of mangrove. Here, too, on Lake Songkhla (see page 116), is some of the kingdom's most spectacular birdlife, including kingfishers, warblers and numerous species of waders.

Nature's gift to Thailand is under pressure, but it has survived and, with the support of wildlife organisations and the awareness of locals and tourists, it may yet live on for future generations to appreciate.

Flowering flame tree

Mountain orchid

Relaxing on a raft in the Kok river

RAFTING

Rafting offers one of the most delightful ways of seeing the countryside for those who have the time and who do not shun the discomfort.

Generally rafts are made from bamboo, tied together with twine and comprise little more than a roof and a floor. During the day they float, or are towed, along the river, while at night they moor on the river bank. You sleep on board or, better still, stay in local villages.

Rafts can be hired in **Kanchana Buri** (see page 68) for a relaxing two days on the **Khwae Noi River** to **Sai Yok National Park**. For an even more fascinating trip, in which you get to see both the countryside and the colourful hilltribes, hire a raft from **Tha Ton** to **Chiang Rai** (see page 86) and take a guide with you. Guides will steer, cook and arrange tours of the villages for the three-day trip. All you need do is appreciate the surroundings and pay the bill.

Because rafts in Tha Ton are made to order, request one at least 3 days in advance of departure.

SAILING

Two coastlines, turquoise seas and uninhabited islands make Thailand ideal for sailing. Boats for hire now cater for every standard, ranging from old-fashioned schooners to world-class racers, and almost all of them offer the comforts and luxury of a five-star cruise.

Most visitors start out from Phuket or Pattaya. Trips last from anything from one day to two weeks and can take you as far as the Similan Islands, the Surin Islands or even to Langkawi and the Malaysian border.

The best time of year for sailing depend on the monsoons. During the rainy season you may find that even the legendary turquoise seas will look an unhealthy grey. The Andaman Sea is best from November to May; the Gulf of Thailand season extends from May to October.

TREKKING TO THE TRIBES

Almost everyone who visits the north will, at some stage, put on their rucksack and walk for anything from a day to a week in search of the nomadic ethnic peoples known as the hilltribes. Many will enjoy it. Some will hate it. Few will discover tribes that have never been seen before.

Trekking in Thailand has become an extremely popular form of adventure travel, involving gentle walks in the countryside, visits to the various hilltribes and boat trips down the rivers. Some up-market treks include elephant rides and even transport in air-conditioned buses.

The primary aim of a trek is to see the tribes, and the best way of doing it is on foot. Spending the night in a village, you will start at dawn, walk perhaps 8km, then stop for lunch before continuing to another village and stopping in the early evening. If you are lucky you may then sit with the tribespeople with your guide acting as interpreter to explain the ways and means of the people. If you are unlucky, you will be placed in a separate hut kitted out for foreigners eating a pot of plastic noodles that your guide has provided.

With countless trekking centres in **Chiang Mai, Chiang Rai** and,

Trekking in northern Thailand has become almost as popular as it is in Nepal

increasingly, **Mae Hong Son**, deciding what sort of trek to choose is no easy matter. Try to check with the tourist authorities for a reliable organisation and talk to other trekkers who have returned from a trip.

Finally, before paying up, find out exactly what is included, how you will be transported back and who will be providing the food. Below is a list of several agencies in Chiang Mai. All the big hotels also run their own more up-market trekking services.

Chiang Mai Honey Tour, *73–4 Charoen Prathet Road (tel: 234 345).*
Siamtours, *123 Chang Klan Road (tel: 274 338).*
The Trekking Collective Company, 25/1 Ratchawithi Road (tel/fax: 66 53 419080).
Youth's International Travel, *252 Phra Pokklao Road (tel: 236 3115).*

Shopping

From teakwood elephants to colourful umbrellas, lacquerware bowls and trendy fashionwear, Thailand offers some of the best buys in one of the best places for shopping in the region.

Indeed shopping has, in many ways, become the country's latest gift to tourists, offering some of the best bargains on offer. Prices suit everyone, from backpacker to big spender.

Do not, however, expect to buy cameras, or for that matter, videos. If those are the sort of goods you are after, better to wait for Hong Kong or Singapore. What Thailand does have is exquisite and well-priced handicrafts along with silks, gems and clothes. In many parts of the country and especially around Chiang Mai, you can actually see the goods being made – lacquerware pots being sprayed by hand or lumps of timber being carved into shapely bowls.

Above all, the thing that characterises shopping in Thailand is the sheer joy of it. Whether you are looking for souvenirs or simply wanting to enjoy a stroll, shopping is fun and provides a fascinating insight into the daily life of the people.

Value for money

Getting value for money is never hard, but squeezing out the last penny can be tiring work. Before asking what the price is, work out how much you are prepared to pay, then bargain hard. Never appear over-anxious to buy and always smile and laugh. Bargaining takes time and trouble. Yet it can be the most rewarding part of shopping.

To get the very best prices always consider buying several articles in one shop and, if possible, compare prices at one place with those in another. Two shops right next to each other may offer vastly different prices. Shopping centres are generally slightly more expensive, but for those who prefer fixed prices they may prove a less perilous alternative.

Markets are normally the best places to buy. But do not dismiss hotel arcades, which generally provide reliable goods at quite reasonable prices.

Lastly a word on fakes. These can be found in many stalls and shops. Some of them are almost as good as the originals. Often it is a matter of luck how long they last. Some people have worn fake Rolex watches for years without trouble, while others have found that theirs packed up after a week. But with very low prices for items such as big-brand watches and pre-recorded cassettes, you are never going to be too disappointed.

To tell a fake watch, feel the weight. To tell fake jeans, feel how thin the cloth is. To tell other fakes just listen to the prices and use your imagination.

Dos and don'ts

Many shops now have a sign on their window resembling an ancient pair of weighing scales. This means it has the approval of the Tourist Authority of Thailand (TAT). That does not always guarantee original goods and it certainly will not give you a price-back guarantee, but it does provide one of the best indicators of a reliable retailer.

Left: basketware is one of the excellent handicrafts you can buy as a souvenir of your visit

Easy and comfortable shopping, Bangkok-style

Ultimately, however, when listening to a gem or antique dealer you must trust your own instincts. Behind the smiles and the charm are some very smart traders. Whatever people tell you, you should always be aware that antiques and Buddha images cannot be taken out of the country without official permission which may not always be forthcoming.

Many shops do, however, offer export services so that you can post your lacquerware elephants directly to your home, either by ship or by air.

The TAT provides a shopping booklet with recommendations. If you have complaints, go and speak to them – although in practice there is little they can do.

Most shops are open between 9.30am and 6pm – and most markets from dawn – but at almost any time you can be sure of finding something that will be open for a spot of last-minute shopping.

ANTIQUES

The oldest thing about antiques is the adage 'don't be taken in by them'. Fakes are many and originals few. Even so, you may discover some real collectors' items, include Ming pottery, Thai and Chinese ivory figures and fabulous old wood carvings. The gradual opening up of Indo-China is also unleashing a wave of products from Burma, Cambodia, Laos, China and Vietnam, including bronze drums, silver figures, carved wood panels and tapestries.

Unless you are an expert, fake or reproduction antiques provide a safer option at much lower prices. Attractive tapestries, old *khon* masks (used in classical Thai dancing) and carved animals are beautifully designed and, what is more, you actually know what you are getting.

There's plenty of choice for souvenirs

Take an exquisitely made *lai* home with you

CLOTHING

In Bangkok, tailors will run up shirts, jackets and skirts in a matter of hours. The quality of workmanship in Thailand may not, however, be as high as in Singapore or Hong Kong, and it pays to shop around.

To start with check out different styles and cuts. If you want a suit or dress tailored make sure you opt for good cloth. Also try to bring an exact copy of what you want as Thai ideas of fashion and those of Westerners can vary widely.

Boutique wear and designer fashion are also rapidly growing industries that have become one of Thailand's biggest sources of export income. Bangkok and Chiang Mai are the best places to pick them up. In Bangkok, try the big shopping centres in **Siam Square** or the **Peninsula Shopping Centre** near the Regent Hotel to get an idea of the immense variety on offer.

Outside that, T-shirts, some fake designer jeans and beachwear are found in abundance almost everywhere and at prices far lower than back home.

HANDICRAFTS

Beautiful handicrafts are a Thai speciality. They range from colourful quilts to leather wallets and artificial flowers. Lacquerware dishes, made from bamboo sprayed with layers of varnish, are especially popular, along with rattan baskets, patterned porcelain jars and stylised dolls. Other perfect gifts, such as the famous hand-painted umbrellas, you can actually watch being made along Chiang Mai's **San Kamphaeng Road** (see page 76).

Busy buying and selling, but mostly counting, at Bo Rai's ruby market

In Bangkok you will find products from all over the region and generally at only marginally higher prices – you will not though, have the feel or the satisfaction of seeing them made.

JEWELLERY

Thailand offers some of the world's keenest prices for precious and semi-precious stones, but only for the real connoisseurs. For those who do not know the ropes, it can prove an expensive education.

Jade, Burmese rubies, blue or black star sapphires and turquoise are what the experts come for. Silver and gold are also popular, with niello-work bracelets often beautifully made and intricately designed with inlaid black alloy.

Often the safest place to buy jewellery is in one of the big hotel boutiques or at a TAT-recommended shop. Never go with a tout, always get a letter of authentication and remember that, for every person who gets a bargain on gems, there are probably four or five who make a loss on them.

THAI SILK

More than any other product, Thailand is associated with silk. The country breeds silkworms, produces yarn, weaves and exports some of the finest silk in the business.

Thai silk tends to have a coarse texture, with an infinite range of colours and a natural filament which makes the resulting fabric crease-free.

Prices vary enormously between the products of the famous **Jim Thompson's**, on Bangkok's Surawong Road, to the smaller boutiques and stalls near by. As a rule silk here is marginally cheaper than in Hong Kong, but more expensive than in India.

Most shops will run up tailor-made designs but, as with clothing in general, take care about cut and design and give them as much time as possible.

WHERE TO BUY

People in Chiang Mai will tell you that silverware, ceramics, painted umbrellas, silk, lacquerware and hilltribe clothing are better there than anywhere else around the country and people in Kanchana Buri that this is the place to buy gems. In Udon Thani and Khon Kaen they will tell you that their silk is best, and in Surin their straw baskets.

Wherever you are, take to heart the saying *caveat emptor* ('let the buyer beware'). Use your own judgement and never believe what touts tell you.

Below is a list of recommended shops for Bangkok and Chiang Mai.

BANGKOK

Antiques
Elephant House, *67/12 Soi Phra Phinit, Soi Suan Phlu, Sathorn Tai Road (tel: 286 5280/2780).*
L'Arcadia, *12/2 Soi 23, Sukhumwit Road (tel: 259 9595/1517).*
Oriental Commercial House Co, *3rd Floor, River City Shopping Complex, Charoen Krung Road (tel: 237 0077 ext 319).*
Prasat Collection, *Peninsula Plaza, 2nd Floor, 153 Ratchadamri Road (tel: 253 9772).*

Intricate, brightly colourful and wonderfully life-like Thai dolls are popular with locals and visitors alike

Thevi, *Oriental Plaza, 1st Floor, Oriental Lane.*

Handicrafts
Bangkok Dolls, *Soi Ratchataphan, Ratchadamri Road (tel: 245 3008).*
Chitrilada Shop, *Oriental Plaza.*
Homemade in Thailand, *45 Soi Pramjan, Sukhumwit 39 (tel: 258 8766).*
Narayana Phand, *127 Ratchadamri Road (tel: 252 4670).*
Tamnan, *Amarin Plaza, 3rd Floor, Phloen Chit Road (tel: 256 9929).*

Gems and semi-precious stones
New Universal, *1144/46 Charoen Krung Road (New Road) (tel: 234 3514).*

Jewellery – but do beware of fakes

Thai Lapidary, *277/122 Rama I Road.*
Uthai Gems, *23/7 Soi Ruam Rudee (tel: 253 8582).*

Tailor-made clothes
Classic Style, *95 Naret Road (tel: 236 1916).*
Perry's, *60/2 Silom Road (tel: 233 9236).*
T Design, *3rd Floor, River City Shopping Complex, Charoen Krung Road (tel: 252 9650).*

Thai cotton and silk
Design Thai, *304 Silom Road (tel: 235 1553).*
Jim Thompson's, *9 Surawong Road (tel: 234 4900).*
Silk Corner, *River City Shopping Complex, 2nd Floor Charoen Krung Road (tel: 237 0077, ask for Silk Corner).*
Thai Shinawatra, *94/23 Sukhumwit Road (tel: 258 0295).*

CHIANG MAI

Antiques
Amaravadee Antiques, *141 Chiangmai-Hod Road (tel: 441 628).*
Banyan, *86/1–3 Wualai Road.*
Borisoothi Antiques, *15/2 San Kamphaeng Road (tel: 331 460).*

Ceramics
Mengrai Kilns, *79/2 Arak Road (tel: 272 063).*
Siam Celadon Factory, *San Kamphaeng Road (tel: 331 526).*

Handicrafts
Arts and Crafts Chiangmai, *172 Mu 2, San Kamphaeng Road (tel: 338 025).*
Boon Lacquerware, *5/2 Mu 6, San Kamphaeng Road (tel: 331 407).*

Beautiful, but expensive, Thai silk

Hilltribe Products Foundation, *21/17 Suthep Road (tel: 221 747).*
Night Bazaar, *Chiang Khlan Road.*
Northern Tribal Crafts, *204/2 Bamrung Rat Road (tel: 245 079).*
Umbrella Making Centre, *111/2 Bor Sang-San Kampaeng Road (tel: 338 324).*

Jewellery and silverware
Lanna Thai, *79 San Kamphaeng Road (tel: 338 015).*
P.N. Precious Stones, *95/4–7 Nimmarnhemin Road (tel: 212 368).*

Thai silk and cotton
Bua Bhat Panich, *147/4–5, Chang Khlan Road (tel: 275 741).*
Chiang Mai Textile and Garment Centre, *56 Mu 3, San Kamphaeng Road (tel: 331 340).*
Parn Chiang Mai, *189/22 Chang Klan Road (tel: 275 119).*
The Loom, *27/3 Ratchamankha Road.*
Shinawatra Thai Silk, *145/1–2km 7, Sankampaeng Road (tel: 338 053).*

Thai markets come in all sorts of shapes and sizes, mostly selling vegetables and fruit, including the extraordinary durian

MARKETS

All the colours, sights and sounds of Thailand are to be found in its markets. They are the traditional commercial hub, the source of wholesale goods and, most of all, a demonstration of the Thai vitality and love of life. Fresh produce arrives after an overnight ride from the provinces, including beautiful flowers still covered in dew, baskets of red and green chillies, hundreds of varieties of banana, pineapple and the strangely scented durian. Live pigs arrive slung over the back of motorbikes along with pots and pans piled to bursting point on the back of trucks and *tuk tuks*.

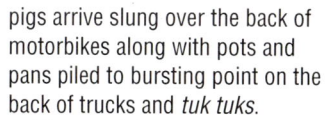

They are joined by tricyclists selling dried squid, locals selling steaming mounds of noodles, beggars, restaurateurs, everyone seemingly with at least some sense of purpose, everything that a photographer hoping to capture the real Thailand could wish for.

Twenty years ago this was the only way to get your produce. Now there are supermarkets, but for the real connoisseurs or those without the money, markets are still the only place to come.

It is not difficult to find a market, all you generally need do is wander down any pavement until you run into a collection of stalls. These normally start trading well before dawn and are at their best before the start of the heat and the dust. Once you are there though, you will not want to leave. Keep a firm grip on your purse or wallet, to safeguard against the danger of pickpockets, and begin the serious business of shopping.

Entertainment

No other country in Asia rivals Thailand when it comes to night-time entertainment. From its bars and boxing to the quieter spectacles of classical dancing, the country outdoes all its competitors. Whether you are alone or in company, a night owl or an early bird, you will always find something worth staying up for.

The best place for nightlife is Bangkok, but Pattaya, Phuket, Chiang Mai and, increasingly, Ko Samui offer various forms of entertainment, boisterous or otherwise.

Bars

Missing out on Patpong would be like coming to Athens and not visiting the Parthenon. Bangkok's world-renowned red-light strip is the most popular single tourist site in the city (see tour on page 32).

For the most part the emphasis is on innocent fun, with the air more of a party than a brothel. Besides the bars and sex shows there are night markets, piled high with a fantastic array of fake goods, restaurants and food stalls – indeed everything that a red-light district generally is not.

When you enter a bar, always check the price of a drink and ask whether there is an entry charge or an entertainment charge. Some upstairs bars are known as clip joints. They will try to charge you an exorbitant price for a drink. If this happens, never struggle or cause a fight. Pay up and immediately report it to the tourist police who are

Night revellers on Patpong Road, Bangkok

ENTERTAINMENT

Huge cinema billboards are a common sight

conveniently situated at either end of the road. They will then accompany you back to the bar and you will get your money back.

Some bars provide other surprises. Bangkok has a growing number of transvestites as well as a special strip for gays. But beware the statistics: AIDS is rapidly increasing and other sexually transmitted diseases are endemic.

Besides Patpong Road, Bangkok has several other red-light districts. Soi Cowboy is situated between Sois 21 and 23, Sukhumwit Road, while the cheaper, raunchier and more down-market Nana Plaza is on Soi 4, Sukhumwit Road.

Cinemas

Cinemas have a prolific concentration both in the capital and throughout the provinces. Most of them are extremely cheap and Thai films contain every conceivable element of violence, romance, religion and comedy all in one. These days, however, there are also plenty of cinemas in Bangkok showing English-language films with Thai subtitles. For details of programmes, check the local newspaper.

Discothèques and live music

Thailand now has some of the largest discos in the world. For a real eye-opener try Bangkok's Nasa Spacedrome with its 3,000-capacity crowds and waitresses dressed in space-age uniforms. A number of the big hotels, such as the Dusit Thani and the Shangri-La, also have their own discos which play a mixture of Thai and Western music.

Bangkok also has excellent rock clubs, a host of jazz bars and occasionally even a string quartet. Details of special performances are given in the *Nation* and the *Bangkok Post* as well as the free distribution magazines found in hotel foyers.

Pubs and hotel bars

That veritable old institution, the English pub, is not forgotten in Thailand. A range of old-worldly, roast-beef-eating, pint-sinking opportunities are there, although mainly in Bangkok, Pattaya and Phuket.

Finally, if that all sounds too much, try the terrace bar at the Oriental Hotel, an idyllic experience, or the Shangri-La Hotel or any other of the quiet hotel cocktail bars on Bangkok's Chao Phraya river. You will not be disappointed.

Night club signs, Pattaya

BANGKOK

Cinemas
Lido Multiplex, *opposite the Siam Centre, Rama I Road (tel: 252 6498)*.
Scala, *Siam Square, Soi 1 (tel: 251 2861)*.
Siam, *Siam Square (tel: 252 7416)*.
Washington, *Sukhumvit Soi 33 (tel: 258 2045)*.

Discos
Bubbles, *Dusit Thani Hotel, Rama IV Road (tel: 236 0450)*.
Freakout, *491/22–24, 1st Floor, Silom Plaza, Silom Road (tel: 234 0972)*.
Nasa, *999 Ramkamhaeng Road, Prakhanong (tel: 314 3368)*.
Talk of the Town, *Shangri-La Hotel, Soi Wat Suan Plu (tel: 236 7777)*.

Go-go bars
Limelight, *86 Patpong 1 Road (Ground Floor)*.
King's Castle, *54/56 Patpong 1 Road (Ground Floor)*.
Goldfinger, *66 Patpong 1 Road (Ground Floor)*.
Queen's Castle, *100 Patpong 1 Road* .

Live music
Blue Moon, *145 Gaysorn Road, Ratchaprasong (tel/fax: 253 7607)*.
Brown Sugar, *231/20 Sarasin Road (tel: 250 0103)*.
Saxaphone, *3/8 Victory Monument, Phya Thai (tel: 246 5472)*.

Pubs
Bobby's Arms, *1st Floor, Carpark, Patpong 2 (tel: 233 6828)*.
Jools, *21/3 Soi Nana Tai, Sukhumvit Road (tel: 252 6413)*.
The Witch's Tavern, *306/1 Soi 55 Sukhumvit. (tel: 391 9791)*.

CHIANG MAI

Bars and pubs
Opium Den, *Chiang Mai Orchid Hotel, Huai Kaeo Road (tel: 222 099)*. Upmarket cocktail bar.
Riverside, *9/11 Charoen Rat Road (tel: 243 239)*. Jazz and meals.
The Pub, *189 Huai Kaeo Road (tel: 211 550)*.
Thaiways Corner & Beer Garden, *117 Khotchasan Road (tel: 232 988)*.

Discos

Bubbles Disco, *Porn Ping Hotel, Charoen Prathet Road (tel: 270 099).*
The Plaza Disco, *Chiang Mai Plaza Hotel, Sri Klon Chai Road (tel: 222 245).*
The Wall Club, *Chiang Inn Hotel, 100 Chang Khlan Road (tel: 270 070).*

Northern Dancing

Old Chiang Mai Cultural Centre, *185/3 Wua Lai Road (tel: 275 097).*

PATTAYA

Bars and Pubs

Garden Bar and Piano Bar, *Royal Cliff Beach Resort (tel: 421 421).* Exclusive, with beautiful views.
Soi Diamond, *south Pattaya.* Biggest concentration of beer and 'go-go' bars.
The Saloon, *Beach Road, south Pattaya.* Genuine live rock 'n' roll.

Cabarets (transvestite)

Alcazar Cabaret, *Pattaya 2 Road (tel: 410 505 or 410 225).*
Tiffany's, *Pattaya Sports Bazaar Building, Pattaya 2 Road (tel: 429 642).*

Discos

Captain's Club, *Dusit Resort, North Pattaya Road (tel: 429 901).*
Pattaya Palladeum, *Pattaya 2 Road, Soi 1 intersection.*
Marine Bar and Discothèque, *South Pattaya Road.*

PHUKET

Bars and pubs

Boathouse Inn, *Kata Beach.* Exclusive. Fine setting.
Doolie's Place, *50/1 Soi Bangla, Patong Beach (tel: 321 209).*
No Idea Cocktail Lounge, *89/49 Soi*

Dancers performing at a winter fair in Lamphun

Post Office, Patong Beach.
Saxaphone, *114/51 Kata Centre, Kata Beach.*

Discos

Banana Disco, *Patong Beach Hotel, Thawiwong Road (tel: 340 301).*
Crocodile Discothèque, *Soi Bangla, Patong Beach (tel: 321 199).*
Marine Disco, *Merlin Phuket Hotel, 7 Yaowarat Road (tel: 212 866).*

Go-Go Girl

Her real name is Nita, although her friends call her Deng. She comes from Khon Kaen, the oldest in a family of seven and she prides herself on being the family breadwinner.

Deng is also one of an estimated 700,000 prostitutes who live and work in the towns and cities of Thailand, plying their bodies to tourists and to locals alike.

Like Deng, many of the girls come from the poor areas of Issan or from the north where life is hard and money difficult to come by. Most of them started work as waitresses or they married, things went wrong, and they joined the ever-growing circle of bargirls.

Deng and her friends work as dancers in the bars or as masseuses in the massage parlours. Many of them send money home to their parents or use it to put their children to a good school so that they may have a better life.

Nobody ignores Deng or the other bargirls, but society looks down on them. Deng is also at great risk of becoming a victim of AIDS. Yet Deng is not unhappy. When she returns home, her friends admire her clothes and other families compliment her parents on having such a good daughter.

Deng is an example of the complex other side of Thai life. For though she is allowed to work openly, she knows that prostitution is illegal and that she is, in theory at least, a criminal.

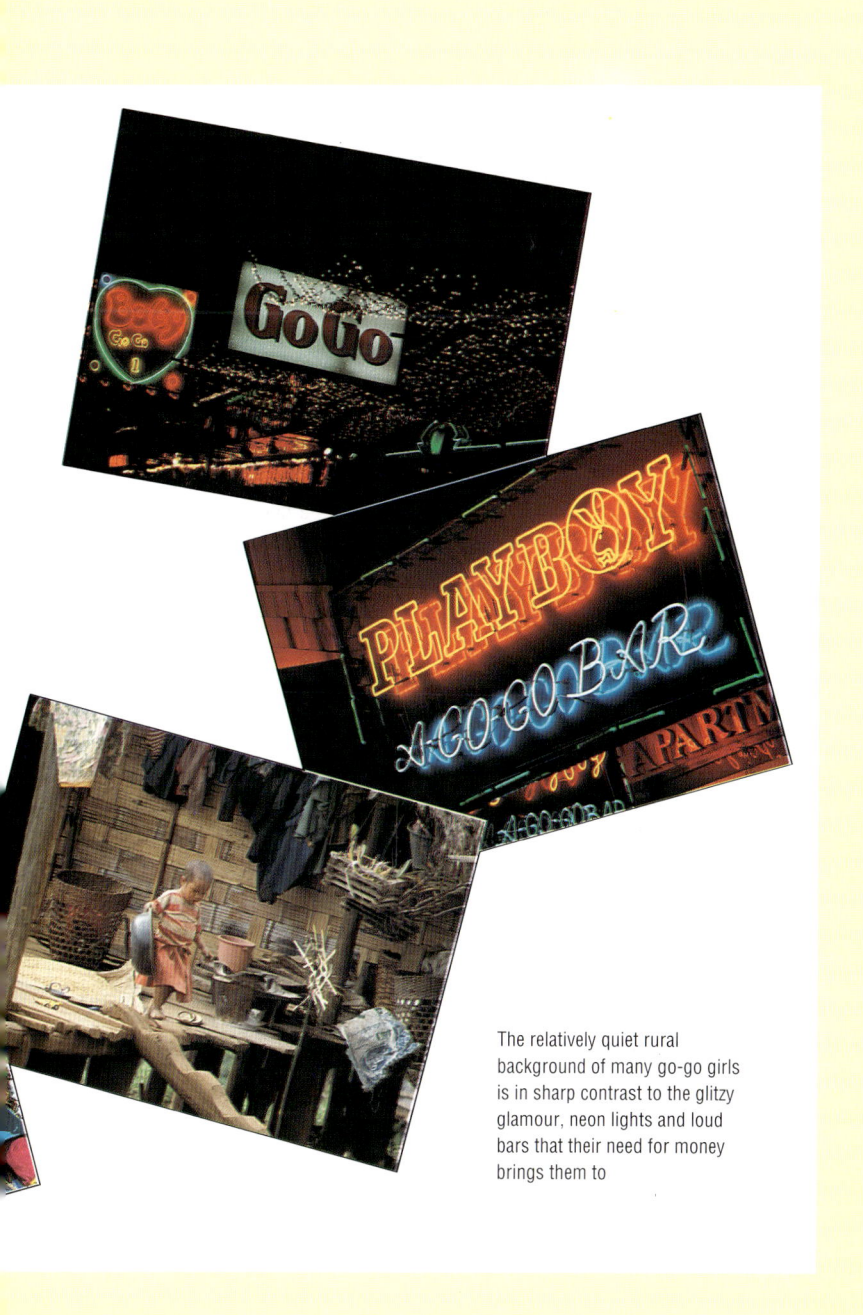

The relatively quiet rural background of many go-go girls is in sharp contrast to the glitzy glamour, neon lights and loud bars that their need for money brings them to

Classic Thai dancing is a delight to watch

THAI DRAMA AND DANCING
Thai classical dancing is a beautiful and exotic spectacle that no visitor should miss.

In the old days, a full performance could take up to a week and include as many as 300 characters, made up of gods, demons, giants, monkeys and angels. These days, it is generally shortened to a couple of hours, highlighting just a few episodes. This is still enough to give an idea both of the rich variety and of the skill involved.

Indeed so complex and demanding are the roles that even the simple use of the fingers (there are some 200 different movements) takes years to perfect. Hardly surprising, then, that most dancers begin training at the age of six and do not go on stage until the age of 15.

Ancient art forms
The dance that most visitors are likely to come across is the masked *khon* dance where the actors wear glittering costumes, covered with gold braid and jewels, as well as magnificent *papier mâché* masks.

Around the country, there are other dances too. In the south, especially, the Manohra dance, which traditionally tells the tale of a half-bird, half-woman, is popular. There is even a derivative known as the 'Flowerpot Dance' introduced during the reign of King Rama I and modified into the 'Lantern Dance' by one of his regal successors.

Story lines
Classical dances almost inevitably come from the famous legend known as the *Ramakien*, which is itself based on the great Hindu *Ramayana* epic. The legend tells of young Prince Rama who is

banished from the kingdom of Ayodhya but, after numerous adventures and the intervention of the monkey King Hanuman, returns triumphantly to his court where, as in all fairy-tales, he lives happily ever after.

You will not get much information from the dancers though. Characters do not speak and only rarely does the scenery change. Even identifying them depends on recognising the colours of the costumes they wear.

There is normally, however, a narrator or chorus that sings along, providing an outline of the plot, and accompanied by a *piphat* (gong and xylophone) orchestra. The music is specifically geared towards the action, with some 200 different tunes each denoting a different mood; one for anger, another for love, a third for betrayal.

Sometimes even that can be hard to absorb. But, as an acquired taste, Thai dancing is said to be like caviar. Once you have got a taste for it you will not want anything else.

PERFORMANCE VENUES IN BANGKOK

National Theatre, *Na Phra That Road* (tel: 224 1342)
Thailand Cultural Centre, *Ratchadaphisek Road, Huai Khwang* (tel: 247 0028)
Sala Rim Naam, *Oriental Hotel, Charoen Nakom Road* (tel: 437 9417)
Baan Thai Restaurant, *7 Sukhumwit Soi 32* (tel: 258 5403).
Maneeya's Lotus Room, *Phloen Chit Road* (tel: 252 6312/0382)
Ruen Thep Restaurant, *Silom Village Trade Centre, Silom Road* (tel: 233 9447, 234 4448).

Candles play a dominant part in many forms of Thai dance and drama

The *likay*

Any account of classical dance would be incomplete without a mention of the *likay*, the indomitable pantomime that sprang up during the reign of King Chulalongkorn.

Whereas classical dance was originally aimed at the aristocracy, *likay* is acted out for the local people. You may see it at a street fair or even at a funeral. Especially popular in rural areas, it tends to be brassy and crude, bawdy and suggestive, but wherever it goes, it continues to captivate the hearts of the people.

In the Candle Festival in Ubon Ratchathani there are floats, food stalls and processions of huge carved candles – human, animal and divine

FESTIVALS

Countless festivals take place during the Thai year ensuring that visitors get at least a chance to share in these delightful national occasions.

Some festivals are local, others national. Whatever they celebrate, the festivities are almost always accompanied by feasts and by dancing, by beauty contests and by unbridled merry-making.

Dates vary from year to year, so always check with offices of the Tourist Authority of Thailand (TAT).

Chiang Mai Flower Festival

Beautiful flower parades and processions held on the first weekend in February when the northern flowers are in full bloom.

Magha Puja

One of the most important Buddhist holidays, held to commemorate the occasion when 1,250 disciples gathered spontaneously to hear the Master preach. Throughout the country candle-lit processions are held around the temples. Celebrated towards the end of February.

Poi Sang Long

Three days of colourful processions to celebrate the ordination of novices progressing to full monkhood. Held at the beginning of April in the northern town of Mae Hong Son.

Pattaya Festival

Pattaya at its most festive with beer, floats, beauty contests and all the other things that the resort is known for. Held in mid-April.

Songkran

The traditional Thai New Year and one of the great annual festivities. People sprinkle water over monks, cover Buddha images with fresh flowers, clean their houses in a symbolic gesture of renewal and fling water everywhere in utmost relish of the nation's lifeblood. The best place to enjoy the excitement of the festivities is Chiang Mai. Held around mid-April.

The Ploughing Ceremony

Sacred bulls are offered a variety of grains. Depending which they eat, seers will forecast the rice crop for the year. Held in Bangkok during early May. Obtain tickets beforehand at the Tourist Authority of Thailand (TAT) office on Ratchadamnoen *(tel: 282 1143)*.

Visakha Puja

The most sacred of all Buddhist days, commemorating the Buddha's birth, enlightenment and death. Beautiful candle-lit processions are held outside the temples. Held at the end of May.

International Swan-Boat Races

Traditional swan-boat racing held on the Chao Phraya river under Bangkok's Rama IX Bridge during September.

ENTERTAINMENT

During the Chak Phra Festival a Buddha image is pulled through Suratthani

Phuket Vegetarian Festival
A 10-day festival in which many of the island's Chinese residents perform extraordinary feats, such as walking on red-hot coals and piercing their skin with spikes, in an effort to cleanse their spirit. Held in October.

Chon Buri Buffalo Races
Buffaloes are let loose around a track with much betting, drinking and local merriment. Held in mid-October.

Surin Elephant Round-Up
A celebration of Thailand's most famous beast. Displays of elephant football, tug-of-war and even boxing. Held in the third week of November. Arrange accommodation well ahead.

Loi Krathong
The most beautiful of all the Thai festivals. People from all over the kingdom make little boats from banana leaves, place a candle and a joss stick inside and launch them on to the rivers and canals in a blaze of colour. The best place to celebrate Loi Krathong is Sukhothai or Chiang Mai. Most of the big hotels in Bangkok also put on special festivities. Held in late October/November.

River Khwae Bridge Week
Light and sound shows and handicraft displays to recall the destruction of the bridge and the so called 'Death Railway' Held in late November/early December.

Trooping of the Colour
Processions held throughout the kingdom to celebrate the king's birthday on 5 December. The best place to be is around Bangkok's Royal Plaza where the Trooping of the Colour starts at around 3pm.

Yok Mub Festival

Children

*B*ringing children to Thailand may seem like hard work, but there are plenty of compensations, such as friendly childminders, excellent hotels and good medical services. There are also plenty of sights to see both in Bangkok and around the country that will appeal to children and to their parents.

Be sure that your children have the necessary injections, provide them with hats and sunglasses, and keep them out of the sun. Apart from these precautions, there is no reason why a visit to Thailand should not be, for them, the holiday of a lifetime.

WHAT TO SEE

BANGKOK AND SURROUNDINGS

Ancient City: Scaled-down models of temples and monuments found throughout the country (see page 66).
Dusit Zoo: More than 500 animals including snakes and elephants (see page 48).
Kite Flying: During spring weekends at Sanam Luang (see page 160).

Native children even ride water buffalo, but it's not recommended for the amateur

Lumphini Park: Pedal boats, walks and ice-creams in the centre of town (see page 53).
Magic Land: *72 Phahon Yothin Road (tel: 513 1731). Open: Monday to Friday 10am–5pm, weekends 10am–7pm. Admission charge.*
Planetarium: *928 Sukhumvit Road (tel: 392 5952). Open: Wednesday to Sunday 9am–4pm, Monday until 2.30pm. Admission charge.*
The Rose Garden: Lush resort to the west of town with daily shows, tribal dances and beautiful gardens (see page 73).

CHIANG MAI AND THE NORTH

Chiang Mai Zoo: Largest zoo in the country (see page 75).
Doi Suthep Temple: Up in the hills with views of Chiang Mai (see page 80).
Mae Sa Valley: Orchid, snake and elephant farms, and waterfalls within easy distance of town (see page 82).

PATTAYA AND THE GULF

Elephant Village: Elephant shows and rides (see page 104).
Khao Khieo Open Zoo: 40 hectares of forest, an aviary, waterfalls and wildlife (see page 105).

Ko Lan Island: Picturesque island with beaches and restaurants reached by boat (see page 104).
Nong Nooch Village: 220 hectares of exotic gardens; daily cultural shows with Thai dancing (see page 105).
Ocean World: Waterslides, wavepool, bumper cars and amusement park. Situated at Bang Saen (see page 106).
Pattaya Park: Big swimming pool, waterchutes and whirlpool within easy reach of Pattaya (see page 105).

PHUKET AND THE SOUTH
Aquarium: Over 100 species of fish on display together with various crustaceans and other marine life (see page 111).
Beaches: Kata and Karon beaches on Phuket (see page 113). Chaweng beach on Ko Samui (see page 123).
James Bond Island: Weird limestone formations and spangled islands at Phang Nga, off Phuket (see page 115).
Nakha Noi Pearl Farm: Home of the largest grown cultured pearl in the world (see page 114).
Mai Khao Beach: The spot where sea turtles come ashore from November to February, to lay their eggs (see page 113).

TEN MAIN ATTRACTIONS FOR CHILDREN

1. Boat trip on Bangkok's Chao Phraya River (see page 28).
2. Bangkok's Snake Farm (see page 56).
3. Crocodile Farm at Samut Prakarn (see page 66).
4. Elephant Farm at Mae Taeng (see page 82–3).
5. Floating Market at Damnoen Saduak (see page 67).
6. Hilltribe village at Ban Doi Pui (see page 80).
7. National Park at Khao Yai (see page 69).
8. Seaside at Phuket (see page 112).
9. Tham Pla ('Fish Cave') at Mae Hong Son (see page 90).
10. Umbrella factories on San Kamphaeng Road, Chiang Mai (see page 76).

You should have no trouble with your children – they are welcome everywhere

Sport

Given the heat, the rain and the humidity, you might think that sport and Thailand were incompatible. In fact neither the elements (nor Bangkok's traffic and pollution) have dinted local appetites for outdoor and indoor exertion.

Golf, tennis and sailing are now so well established that new clubs are even taking precedence over traditional sports, while even in the heat of a Bangkok evening, crowds can be seen running around the parks, pulling tyres and practising tae kwon do (martial arts).

FITNESS CENTRES

Fitness centres, weight rooms and saunas are found in most big hotels. Bangkok, especially, offers plenty of choice. The **Dusit Thani Hotel** on *Rama IV Road (tel: 236 0450)*, the **Menam Hotel** on *Charoen Krung Road (tel: 289 1148)* and the **Landmark Hotel** on *Sukhumvit Road (tel: 254 0404)* all have facilities open to non-hotel guests. The **Oriental Hotel** *(tel: 236 0400)*, **Shangri-La Hotel** *(tel: 236 7777)* and the **Siam InterContinental Hotel** *(tel: 253 0355)* have gyms reserved for hotel guests only.

Outside Bangkok a number of resorts and hotels also have facilities, especially in Phuket and Pattaya. Enquire at offices of the Tourist Authority of Thailand (TAT) for details.

Golf courses are now well laid-out and cared for – a far cry from the days when you could find tiger prints in the bunkers

GOLF

One of the great newly discovered paradises for golfers, Thailand's greens are now attracting the sort of attention that only a few years ago was reserved for its beaches. Its secret? Good weather, challenging courses, cheap caddies, low fees and easy access.

In all, the country has more than 50 courses. Generally these will rent out golf clubs and balls, although you should always check before you leave home.

Local courses within reach of Bangkok are the **Navatanee** *(tel: 376 1687)*, **Krungthep Kritha** *(tel: 379 3716)*, the **Rose Garden** *(tel: 322 769)* and **Unico** *(tel: 377 9038)*. Outside Bangkok some of the best golf courses are the **Royal Hua Hin Golf Course** at Hua Hin *(tel: (032) 512 475)*, the **Lanna Golf Club** in Chiang Mai *(tel: (053) 221 743)* and the **Phuket Golf and Country Club** at Phuket *(tel: (076) 321 038)*.

Weekday rates range from bt350 to bt2,500 for a round of 18 holes, although costs are higher at weekends. Caddies generally cost in the region of bt200. Most clubs have restaurants, bars and often accommodation. Always book in advance, especially at weekends when clubs are most popular.

HORSE RACING

Unexpected it may be, but Bangkok has two full-sized racing courses. This may have more to do with the Thai propensity for betting than with their love of horses, but it is enough to make horse racing especially popular. Races take place at the **Royal Turf Club** at *183 Phitsanulok Road (tel: 280 0020)* and at the **Royal Bangkok Sports Club** *(tel: 251 0181)* on alternate Sundays. Both clubs have membership enclosures.

In *takraw* you have to keep a rattan ball aloft using any part of the body except the hands – the Thai national pastime

Outside, there are also public stands, where the gambling can be seen.

For those wanting to ride, the main centres outside Bangkok are the **Phuket Riding Club**, *Viset Road, Kauon Beach (tel: 076 381 667)* and **Pattaya's Reo Ranch** which offers 6km of trail-rides on thoroughbreds imported from Australia.

SWIMMING AND TENNIS

For a splash you will not need to go far. All the big hotels have swimming pools and even the medium-sized hotels have small pools. Outside that there are few public baths save for Bangkok's **YMCA** *(tel: 287 2727)* at 27 Sathorn Tai Road which is open daily 7am–7pm.

For tennis courts try Bangkok's **Ambassador Hotel**, the **Shangri-La Hotel** and the **Imperial Hotel** as well as the Central Tennis Courts at *13/1 Soi Attakarnprasit, Sathorn Tai Road (tel: 286 7202)* and *Soi Klang Racquet Club, 8 Soi 49, Sukhumvit*.

TRADITIONAL THAI SPORTS

From Thai-style boxing to fighting fish and kite-flying, the Thais appear to have an unquenchable relish for obscure athletic and spectator sports. The origin of some of these sports can be traced back centuries, and they remain a strong form of local entertainment and are a major source of betting.

FIGHTING FISH

This is not really a sport, nor is it even legal, but fighting fish (the species *Bettas spendens*) continue to provide one of the most popular and unusual activities in the country. The game begins when two males are put together in a tank or basin after bets have been taken.

The fight can last for seconds or for hours and only comes to an end when one of the fish dies or flees to a corner. Although officially banned in Thailand, fights can be widely seen. Elsewhere, cricket fights, bullfights and cockfights attract an equal outpouring of bets.

KITE-FLYING

When the skies are clear and the wind is up, the popular kite-flying season gets underway.

Most fliers participate in a competition, the aim of which is to try and snare the line of an opponent's kite with their own and then pull the enemy kite across a capture line marked on the ground.

At weekends, especially between February and April, **Sanam Luang**, opposite Bangkok's Grand Palace, is a solid mass of colours as kites of all different shapes and sizes bob around the sky. Occasionally Thailand even holds international competitions to find the world's best kite-flier.

LONGBOAT RACING

Longboat racing, one of the country's oldest sports, dates back to the Ayutthaya period (14th to 18th century) and can still be seen, although these days only on a few occasions. Races are held under Bangkok's Rama IX Bridge on the Chao Phraya River, normally in September. In the provinces, the towns of Nan, Nakon Phanom and Phi Mai also hold their own races scheduled between the months of September and November.

MUAY-THAI

This is the most popular spectator sport in Thailand and the biggest crowd-puller in the capital. *Muay-Thai*, or Thai-style boxing, has not become a big hit without good reason.

Like normal boxing, it involves two opponents wearing gloves but, unlike normal boxing, competitors can use their feet, fists, knees and elbows to batter each other into submission. Bouts consist of five three-minute rounds accompanied by music and frantic betting, especially among the third-class ticket holders.

Left: hundreds of kites wait to fly and fight every weekend in spring

A longboat race at Nan

Such is the demand that there are normally at least 10 bouts in any night's programme.

Thai boxing is held in Bangkok at the **Ratchadamnoen Stadium** *(tel: 281 4205) Ratchadamnoen Nok Avenue* on Mondays, Wednesdays, Thursdays and Sundays or at Lumphini Boxing Stadium *(tel: 251 4303)* on *Rama IV Road near park*. Prices range from bt150 for third-class seats to over bt1,000 for a top ringside seat. Seats are generally available on the night and do not require booking.

TAKRAW – RATTAN BALLGAME

This popular sport is played everywhere. Requiring great skill, it uses a small, hollow rattan ball. Players must neither touch the ball with their hands, nor allow it to touch the ground. Elbows, shoulders, the back of the head can be used. The more complicated the feat, the better the score. Played by six to seven men, a version known as *hoop takraw* is the most popular. During a 30-minute game, each man co-operates with another in order to earn a high score. Played without nets or hoops, the ball passes from player to player and each scores according to his dexterity. Net *takraw* matches can be seen at the National Stadium in Bangkok. In the country you will see people playing it after work.

TRADITIONAL MASSAGE

Tense? Exhausted? A traditional massage could be just the thing. Thai massage traces its roots back hundreds of years, owes its existence to the great Indian civilisation and involves applying pressure to certain points within the body.

To experience it as it should be, visit **Wat Pho** (see page 58), the home of traditional massage. Other places in Bangkok include the **Marble House** at *37/18 Soi Surawong Plaza (tel: 235 3519)* and **Buathip Thai Massage** at *4/13 Sukhumwit Soi 5 opposite the Landmark Hotel (tel: 255 1045)*.

Outside these veritable establishments massage tends to be less traditional and more costly.

WATERSPORTS

Once sand and blue seas were enough to attract visitors to Thailand. Now it is the things that go with them: the parasailing and game-fishing, the sailing and waterskiing. These are aimed at visitors of all skill levels, and in all price ranges, and can be arranged either by your hotel or on the beach itself.

Main centres are Phuket and Pattaya. Increasingly Ko Samui, Krabi and Ko Phi Phi are beginning to offer more extensive facilities. Wherever you are, and whatever people tell you to the contrary, always check on safety standards and always ask for official certification. It may not be much, but it could just save your skin.

DEEP-SEA FISHING

Increasingly popular, deep-sea fishing is now available in many forms to suit the amateur or the specialist. The best centres are Pattaya and Jomtien, where catches range from blue marlin to barracuda. When you have hooked your fish, you can take it to a nearby restaurant, where they will turn it into some local delicacy. Enquire at the **Bang Saray Fisherman's Lodge** in Bangkok *(tel: 436 069)* or the **Game Fishing Club**, Pattaya *(tel: (038) 429 645)*.

PARAGLIDING

Paragliding, the sport of jumping into the air behind a speed-boat suspended from a kite, may not be everyone's idea of fun, but it is the latest hit sport to come Thailand's way. Almost all the big island resorts now offer facilities; indeed, in Pattaya and on Phuket's Patong Beach, paragliding is so popular that people just wanting to sunbathe or paddle hardly get a look in.

Official instructors will show you the ropes. Be warned, however, that there have been accidents. Check out the situation before you get up there.

SAILING

From 30m sailing cruisers and catamarans to small hobbies and dinghies, Thailand has just about every form of motorised, sail-based and oar-propelled water transport. The big centres are Phuket and Pattaya. Make sure that you book in advance, especially during the high season. The following organise trips: **Ease West Siam** at *70/176 Paradise Complex, Rat-U-Thit Road, Patong Beach (tel: 340 912/341 188)*; **Thai Yachting**, *94/97–98 Thaveewong Road, Patong Beach (tel: 341 153)*.

SCUBA DIVING

Visitors who come to Thailand specifically to dive may still be in the minority, but they represent a growing number. The chief destinations are Phuket, Pattaya and Krabi, although the

All sports are popular in the jet-set resorts of Pattaya and Phuket

The clear turquoise waters off Phuket are perfect for scuba-diving

lesser known Similan and Surin Islands also offer colourful coral reefs and underwater marine life. Good sheltered water is generally found around the islands at any time of year (although during the monsoon the water becomes cloudy) and boats are readily available to take you out there. For those with no previous experience, scuba-diving courses are offered at Phuket and Pattaya; as well as catering for beginners there are also courses for advanced divers. Alternatively equipment can be hired at numerous shops along the beach. For those with lesser ambitions, snorkels and face masks are also widely available. The best months for diving near Phuket are November to April. From June to November during the southwest monsoon, the area can be tricky and visibility poor.

The following firms hire out equipment and offer diving instruction: **Ocean Divers**, *Patong Beach, Phuket (tel: (076) 341 273);* **Andaman Divers**, *Patong Beach, Phuket (tel: (076) 341 126);* **Samui International Diving School**, *Ko Samui (tel: (077) 422 386).*

WINDSURFING

Windsurfers who come to Thailand will not find the surf of Kuta Beach, nor the boards of Hawai, but windsurfing is on the increase and popular spots are to be found in Jomtien, Phuket and Ko Samui. Windsurfing boards can be rented on a daily basis. Enquire at any of the beaches for details.

Food and Drink

To the great culinary nations of the world there has been added a new and rising star. Thailand is no longer just a third-world market stall, but an experience for connoisseurs, with new Thai restaurants springing up in large numbers around the world, as well as recipe books and cooking courses taking up its cause.

Thai food encapsulates an enormous variety of tastes and spices ranging from the glutinous rice of the northeast to the pungent curries of the south. It brings together some of the finest cooking traditions from all over Asia. Above all it is a celebration by people who love their food and who count eating as being one of the great pleasures in life.

A selection of Thai vegetables and spices

A touch of spice

Thai food can be spicy or mild, but it is never purely and simply hot. Numerous spices are used to enhance the flavour and to improve the taste, but never to conceal it.

The blend of ingredients partly reflects the historical mix of the people themselves. Thai food is a combination of various cuisines, including Indian, Malay, Chinese and Indonesian.

The most important spice for any dish is chilli. *Phrik lueng* is the hottest chilli, despite its lovely yellow-orange colour. *Phrik khi nu* is not so potent while *phrik yuak* and *phrik chi fa* are relatively mild.

But there is far more to Thai cooking than chillies. Coriander is sprinkled on meats, along with garlic and pepper, to enhance the taste. Ginger and tamarind add further flavour along with mint, basil, cardamom and galanga.

Lemongrass, a spice used extensively in soups and salads adds a certain piquancy, while many dishes use coconut milk and pineapple, adding a mellowness, cooling the palate and complementing the other spices.

Playing the gourmet

About the one requirement demanded by Thai food is that you should enjoy it. Beyond that, eat it how you want, when you want and with what you want. There is no need for knives nor even for bowls and if you swallow a chilli, don't worry about convention – just dive for the rice bowl or a glass of water.

Thais do, however, follow a few guidelines. Almost always they order a selection of dishes and share them together. As an accompaniment they will almost always have rice. In principle they will choose a balanced range of dishes including fish, meat, curry and vegetables.

Finally, you will find that locals generally wash down a good Thai meal with either mekong (rice-based) whisky or beer, but rarely wine. Vintage wine is considered extravagant and ill-suited for the flavours of Thai food. Generally a bottle would also cost more than the whole meal.

A typical menu

A typical menu will usually include a *tom yam* (hot) soup, a spicy salad *(yam)*, a curry *(gaeng)* and a fried fish *(pla tod)*. For variety there may be a chicken in pandanus leaves *(gai haw bai toey)* as well as a coconut-based broth *(tom ka gai)* and some fried vegetables *(phak phat ruam mit)*.

It would be a waste not to try the seafood at the coastal resorts

For those who like food untarnished by chillies, ask for *mai phet* (not hot). Order a sweet-and-sour fish *(pla priew wan)* or roast duck *(phet tod)*, some noodles *(mi crop)* or a plate of fried rice with chicken *(khao phat kai)*.

For dessert, the Thais favour dishes which foreigners often find excessively sweet. They are called *khanom* and may vary from riceflour and coconut milk to sticky rice and custard. If you do not have a sweet tooth it is safer to ask for *pollamai* (fresh fruits) and eat bananas, pineapples or the strange fruit *mangosteen*.

Other cuisines

Excellent Thai food there may be in abundance, but that does not stop those with a taste for other foods from enjoying excellent Chinese, Vietnamese and European-style cuisine.

These restaurants are now found throughout Bangkok as well as in Chiang Mai, Phuket and Pattaya.

Ducks are a popular delicacy

The local touch

A sense of adventure and an expectation of the unusual are two qualities that any potential diner should have.

For Thais enjoy several dishes which as yet go unappreciated by the Western palate. Snake's blood is one of the most consummate delicacies. The blood of cobras, kraits and vipers, served up by mobile snake shops at Lumphini Park is not only delicious, but is said to be the secret of eternal life and vitality.

Mouse and fried grasshoppers also provide wholesome snacks, while water buffalo is eaten almost everywhere, even in many restaurants around Bangkok.

Finally there is another delicacy that you should not turn your nose up at. Waterbeetles, of the type known as *mengphu*, are especially prized. Eaten raw (but only the female) three can cost as much as bt20 – but such is their quality, that they are considered a meal in themselves.

Going regional

Wherever you go in Thailand you are likely to get curry, *tom yam* soup or the omniscient *khao phat kai* (fried rice). But some areas are particularly renowned for their regional specialities.

Anyone visiting the northeast has to try *larb*, a dish made from water buffalo,

Sometimes a strong stomach is called for

pork or beef, fried with garlic, chillies and shallots and served with cabbage and mint, or with *khao niao*, a form of glutinous rice. Also not to be missed is *somtam*, made from shredded green mango, dried shrimps, lemon juice, garlic and chilli – the perfect antidote to any cold.

In the deep south, food tends to be hotter, with such ferociously piquant dishes as *kaeng lueang* (yellow curry) and *kaeng tai pla* (fish kidney curry). If you do not like hot foods it is safer to opt for fresh prawns, seafood cooked in coconut milk or Phuket lobster.

Khantoke dinners

Visitors to Chiang Mai may well find themselves confronted, at some stage, with the dinner known as *khantoke*. This is a traditional banquet comprising several dishes, including a thick pork curry spiced with garlic and ginger, minced pork cooked with tomatoes and chillies, fried pork skin, chicken and vegetable curry and minced meat mixed with chillies. It is delicious.

Street stalls

An indefinable urge, combined with an almost unheard of terror, generally grips most people when they stare at a wagon loaded with succulent grilled kebabs.

But it is here that you will find some of the best regional and local food; luscious pieces of chicken or steaming bowls of noodles, piping-hot soups with fish, or tangy sausages flavoured with herbs and pork and stuffed with rice.

Do not ignore them. Although you should go easy on the stomach, especially in the first few days of your visit, be aware that these are some of the best, cheapest and most delicious foods that Thailand has on offer.

Thais have no taste for wine; mostly they drink rice whisky. Have a care if you're not used to it

Fruits

Whatever time of the year you are in Thailand, you will come across some of the most sumptuous and exotic fruits in the world. The most prized is the durian, a fruit that resembles a green hedgehog, and smells like a rubbish tip but tastes great. Then there are pineapples and coconuts, papayas and mangoes along with the sweet translucent flesh of rambutans and small sweet custard apples. Finally there are grapes, strawberries, apples, more than 10 kinds of banana and even a type of tangerine known as *som* which is widely grown.

LIQUID REFRESHMENTS

Almost all drinks that are available in the West can be found in Thailand. Water is bought in bottles although restaurants and cafés will almost always boil their own. The two local beers, Kloster and Singha, are quite palatable. Wine is available in the more up-market restaurants but at very high prices. The most popular drink in the land is *mekong*, a rice-based whisky, which does indescribable things to your head.

WHERE TO EAT

Eating in Thailand is usually very cheap. A good Thai meal will generally cost less than bt350 a head (excluding alchohol). Only if you eat in European restaurants in the big hotels will the cost be much higher.

In the restaurant listings below the following symbols have been used to indicate the average cost per person, not including alcohol:
BT1 = bt100–bt250
BT2 = bt250–bt350
BT3 = bt350–bt650

Service is generally charged at the rate of 10 per cent in the bigger restaurants. Outside that it is generally sufficient to leave bt30 on the table.

Thai food – fresh ingredients and spices

BANGKOK

Thai food
Bussaracum BT3. *35 Soi Pipat, off Convent Road (tel: 235 8915)*. One of Bangkok's best-known classical Thai restaurants.
Sala Rim Nam BT3. *Oriental Hotel, Charoen Krung Road (tel: 437 9417)*. Exclusive dining by the river with classical dancing.
Silom Village (Ruen Thep) BT2. *286 Silom Road (tel: 234 4448)*. Good food and gamelan (gong) music within easy reach of shops.
Tanying BT2. *10 Pramuan Road, Silom (tel: 236 4361)*. Good Thai cuisine in beautifully decorated house.
Tum Nak Thai BT1. *131 Ratchada Phisek Road (tel: 274 6420)*. The world's largest restaurant with Thai classical dancers and over 500 dishes.
Whole Earth Restaurant BT1. *93/3 Soi Langsuan, Phloen Chit Road (tel: 258 4900)*. Vegetarian and Thai food to the sound of classical guitar.

International food
La Normandie BT3. *Oriental Hotel, Charoen Krung Road (tel: 234 8690)*. Most expensive and exclusive French food in town.
El Gordo's BT2. *130/8 Soi 8 Silom Road (tel: 234 5470)*. Best Mexican restaurant in town.
Haus Muenchen BT2. *4 Sukhumvit 15 (tel: 252 5776)*. German specialities.
Le Banyan BT3. *59 Sukhumvit Soi 8 (tel: 253 5556)*. Classic French restaurant.
L'Opera BT3. *53 Sukhumvit Soi 39 (tel: 258 5606)*. Top Italian specialities.

Floating restaurants
Pearl of Siam BT3. Operated by *Shangri-La Hotel (tel: 255 9200)*. Nightly candle-lit dinner cruises.
Tahsaneeya Nava (Loy Nava) BT2 *(tel: 437 4932)*. One of the oldest and most elegant riverside restaurants.

CHIANG MAI

Thai food
Baan Suan Restaurant BT2. *51/3 San Kamphaeng Road (tel: 242 116)*.

Delicious food, delightful grounds.
Riverside Bar and Restaurant BT2.
9/11 Charoen Rat Road (tel: 243 239).
Thai and European food, live bands.
Sawairiang BT2. *Chiang Mai Lakeside Ville, 308 Nongphung Soi 8, Chiang Mai-Lamphun Road (tel: 510 0258).* Excellent food in rural atmosphere.
Whole Earth Restaurant BT2. *88 Sridonchai Road (tel: 282 463).* Vegetarian and northern food in teak house.

Khantoke dinners
Banquets in the northern style (see page 167).
Old Chiang Mai Cultural Centre BT3. *185/3 Wua Lai Road (tel: 275 097).*
Diamond Hotel BT3. *33/10 Charoen Prathet Road (tel: 272 080).*

International food
Alt Heidelberg BT2. *96/17 Huai Kaeo Road (tel: 222 034).* German food.
Balcony Restaurant BT1. *40 Bamroongburi Road (tel: 221 538).* Thai and Western specialities.
Café de Paris BT2. *14/16 Khotchasan Road, near Thaphae Gate (tel: 274 804).* Best French cuisine.
Kai Thong Restaurant BT1. *67 Khotchasan Road (tel: 276 584).* Jungle specialities including snake and boar.

PATTAYA

Thai Food
Dolf Riks Restaurant BT2. *Regent Mariana Complex, North Pattaya (tel: 428 569).* Best-known restaurant in town.
PIC Kitchen BT2. *Soi 5, Beach Road, North Pattaya (tel: 428 387).* Tropical gardens. Excellent Thai food.
Ruen Thai BT2. *485/3 Pattaya 2 Road (tel: 425 911).* Traditional Thai restaurant with classical dancing.

International food
El Toro Steakhouse BT2. *214/31–32, Pattaya 2 Road (tel: 426 238).* A good selection of steaks and hors-d'oeuvres is served here.
La Gritta BT2. *North Beach Road (tel: 428 161).* Authentic Italian food accompanied by pianist.
Lobster Pot BT1
228 Beach Road, opposite Soi 14 (tel: 426 083). Seafood served from old fishermen's wharf.
Noble House Restaurant BT2. *310 Beach Road South (tel: 423 630).* A varied selection of European, Thai and Chinese dishes.

PHUKET

Thai food
Ban Rim Pa BT3. *100/7 Kalim Beach Road, Patong Beach (tel: (076) 340 789).* Traditional teak house with top gourmet cooking.
Kan Eang 1 BT2. *9/3 Chaofa Road, Chalong Bay (tel: 381 323).* One of Phuket's best fish restaurants with first-class views.
Tunk-ka Café BT3. *Khao Rang Hill, Phuket Town (tel: 211 500).* Japanese and Thai seafood specialities with beautiful views.

International food
Buffalo Steak House BT2. *Soi 94/25, Patong Beach.*
Le Jardin BT2. *Soi Bangkla, Patong Beach (tel: 340 391).* Good French food in the heart of the night scene.
Pizzeria Napoli BT1. *Soi Post Office, Patong Beach.* Italian restaurant offering pizzas and spaghetti.
Vecchia Venezia BT2. *82/16 Soi Bangla, Patong Beach.* Good seafood and charming ambience.

Hotels and Accommodation

Thailand is justifiably ranked as having some of the finest hotels in the world. Names like the Oriental, the Royal Orchid Sheraton and the Shangri-La now pop up regularly amongst the top international reviews, and are just as pricey as elsewhere. But the characteristic *namchai* (hospitality) does not necessarily stop in the top slot. Numerous smaller and cheaper establishments offer the sort of service that, in the West, would cost an arm and leg – and even the backpacker is not forgotten.

Most visitors book their accommodation prior to departure, but before signing on the dotted line, find out exactly what you are in for. Hotels may have swimming pools and restaurants, but if they are a long way from the centre you could find your movements unbearably restricted, bearing in mind Thai traffic jams. Those who do not book a room prior to arrival can generally find the full range of accommodation on offer (and generally at cheaper rates than back home). At some times of year, however, a reservation is a definite advantage, if not a must. In Phuket and Ko Samui during Christmas and the New Year hotels are reserved months in advance.

Dos and don'ts

Room prices in Thailand usually include a 10–15 per cent service charge and 7 per cent tax, although you should always enquire before you book.

During the low season (March to September) hotels may offer special rates. Some international travel agencies these days are also able to offer very substantial discounts, either as part of a package tour or for a short stopover on the way to some other Asian destination.

Bear in mind the following points when selecting your hotel. Stay clear of hotels situated next to a building site or on a main road, especially in Bangkok, but these days in Phuket and Pattaya as well. Be wary of hotels undergoing renovation (workmen are at it 24 hours a day) and those establishments which double up as brothels (a less trustworthy breed of clientele).

Do not drink tap water. Big hotels provide mineral water in fridges, cheaper hotels jugs of boiled water. Tip the staff if they provide excellent service or if you are staying in a luxury hotel, but remember that bt20–50 is normally quite ample. Always check that your door or window is secure and, if you are staying in a bungalow, bring a padlock.

Finally remember that phone calls and hotel meals are expensive. Also put things in perspective: hotels in Bangkok may provide a pleasant interlude, but the real Thailand is generally found outside, in the streets and market stalls and in the delightful little restaurants.

Off the beaten track

When you are off the main tourist routes do not expect to find the same sort of accommodation that you would find in the major tourist centres. In small towns, hotels may be located in beautiful old Chinese wooden houses. Others double up as brothels. Sometimes there is no choice at all.

To make things easier, always try to arrive in a place during daylight. The moment you arrive start looking around. If you are stuck for accommodation ask at the police station *(satanee tamruat)* or

The luxurious Hotel Dusit Island Inn, Chiang Rai

The Wang Yom Resort in Si Satchanalai

at the bus station. If you are still stuck, go to the local *wat* (temple), ask for permission to stay and leave a donation.

Remember that the word for hotel is *rong raem* and for guest house *gue how* (similar to the English words but Thais find it difficult to pronounce 'st').

In general, you should be able to find some sort of accommodation almost anywhere, though it may not be what you want and it may not have a private bathroom. But if that bothers you, you should stay in one of the main centres.

Prices and facilities

What you get for your money is likely to depend as much on when you come as how you arrange it. During the popular tourist months, from November through

Budget accommodation in Ban Phu

to February, room rates are generally around 20 per cent higher, although it is always worth checking out several agents and hotels.

Four- and five-star accommodation
Top-quality hotels in Thailand offer all the amenities that you would find anywhere in the world. Fine restaurants, discothèques, cocktail lounges and other entertainment facilities are generally provided, along with business facilities, fax services and IDD telephones. Some hotels provide special secretarial services and almost all of them have 24-hour room service.

The luxury hotel sector is the one that has grown fastest in recent years. In theory that should mean cheaper rates, although this has yet to be reflected in prices.

Rooms at the **Oriental**, Bangkok's best-known riverside hotel, range from a normal room to the Royal Suite and accordingly room rates vary greatly. At the nearby **Shangri-La** prices are slightly lower and, as with most hotel room rates in Bangkok, are often quoted in US dollars.

Hotels outside Bangkok tend to be cheaper, with an excellent standard of accommodation in Chiang Mai, Chiang Rai, the Golden Triangle, Mae Hong Son, Phuket, Ko Samui and Pattaya.

Any luxury hotel should be able to advise you on tours as well as arranging chauffeurs, transfer to the airport or any other travel requirement.

Amari Hotels and Resorts offer a range of good-value, four-star accommodation to suit both business and leisure travellers. They have four hotels in Bangkok, one in Chiang Mai, three beach resorts in Pattaya, Phuket and Samui and a mountain resort in northern Thailand.

Standard accommodation
General standards of hotels in the middle group are high, prices are relatively

cheap, while the food and service are more than adequate – though without the attention to detail that is found in the more uppercrust establishments.

Most of the hotels in this range offer swimming pools as well as a restaurant, bar, travel desk and room service. Rooms are air conditioned and almost all have safes where you can leave your valuables.

Prices in Bangkok vary from bt850 at the **YMCA** to bt3,000 at the upmarket **Narai Hotel**. In the provinces, or on the islands, standard accommodation offers good, clean and (by Western standards) exceptionally cheap rooms. This is especially true of Ko Samui with good bungalows costing upwards of bt500. In Phuket standard accommodation tends to cost considerably more.

Budget accommodation

One thing Thailand does not lack is cheap accommodation. Small rooms in big hotels, grubby rooms in grubby hotels, spartan guest houses, private homes – all these cater to the largest tourist grouping: the budget traveller.

Budget accommodation in Bangkok begins at **Khao San Road**, the backpacker's street, in downtown Banglampoo, that has become known the world over. A bed in a dormitory can be had for as little as bt80 and single rooms for upwards of bt100. Most of the guest houses have communal bathrooms and small restaurants, although the vast number of such places means that there is generally something to suit every need.

More up-market versions of Khao San Road are found throughout Bangkok, though at generally higher prices. One of the most popular establishments at the top end of the range is the **Malaysia Hotel** with prices ranging from bt500.

In the provinces, prices for a room in a guest house start at around bt100, although you may have to pay considerably more in Phuket. Theft from budget accommodation is by no means unknown. Always take precautions, not only against outsiders, but also against your fellow travellers.

Inside the Thai Yun Yong Hotel

Practical Guide

CONTENTS
Arriving
Camping
Children
Climate
Clothing
Crime
Customs Regulations
Travellers with Disabilities
Driving
Drugs
Electricity
Embassies and Consulates
Emergency Telephone Numbers
Etiquette
Health
Hitch-hiking
Insurance
Language
Lost Property
Maps
Measurements and Sizes
Media
Money Matters
National Holidays
Opening Hours
Organised Tours
Pharmacies
Photography
Places of Worship
Police
Post Offices
Public Transport
Student and Youth Travel
Telephones
Time
Tipping
Toilets
Tourist Offices
Valeting/Laundry
What to Take

ARRIVING
Entry formalities

Visitors from most countries will need a visa to stay in Thailand for more than 30 days. All passports must be valid for at least six months beyond the date of departure from Thailand.

Visas may also be issued for 30 days (transit visa), for 60 days (tourist visa) and for 90 days (non-immigrant visa). They are obtainable from all Thai embassies and consulates abroad.

Extensions of tourist and non-immigrant visas can be requested at the Immigration Division, Bangkok or at other immigration centres throughout the country. Travellers staying for less than 30 days without a visa must be in possession of confirmed onward/return air tickets. Anyone overstaying their visa is fined bt100 per day.

By air

Bangkok's Don Muang International Airport is served by more than 40 airlines with frequent flights to and from Europe, North America and Australia. International flights and charter companies also serve Phuket, Hat Yai and Chiang Mai.

Standards of efficiency at Don Muang are high, both at the airport (which has a duty-free shop) and at Thai International, the national carrier.

Remember to book flights well in advance. Over Christmas flights are often booked six months in advance. Airport tax of bt200 is charged on departure for international flights.

The Thomas Cook Worldwide Network Licensee (see page 190) will offer airline ticket re-routing and revalidation to travellers who have purchased their travel tickets from Thomas Cook.

To and from the airport

To get from Don Muang International Airport to Bangkok, which is situated some 22km away (average journey time: 90 minutes), catch one of the airport taxis whose drivers wait in the lobby in the arrivals hall. These registered taxis are the form of transport recommended by the tourist authority. Thai Limousine Service is more expensive, but luxurious. Shuttle buses and ordinary buses also run to the big hotels and the centre.

Trains leave infrequently to Hualamphong Railway Station but, if you have luggage, it is hardly worth the trouble. Finally, avoid touts who offer to take you independently to your hotel.

To contact the airport: *(tel: 535 1254)*. Information about arrivals and departures is available 24 hours a day. Lists of airline telephone numbers can be found in most of the free local handout magazines and in the English-language *Yellow Pages* phone directory.

By rail

Trains link Singapore and Bangkok, with intermediate stops at Kuala Lumpur and Butterworth in Malaysia, and at the southern Thai towns of Hat Yai and Suratthani (jump-off point for Ko Samui). Journey times from Singapore to Bangkok are approximately 36 hours and from Butterworth to Bangkok 20 hours.

Sleepers are available, although you should reserve in advance. At the Malaysian border all passengers must alight to go through immigration.

All trains depart and arrive at Hualamphong Station on *Rama IV Road*

Flights are operated efficiently and reasonably by Thai Airways International

(tel: 223 7010 or 223 7020) where there is also a booking office. Advanced tickets can be purchased at all principal stations or the Bangkok Advanced Booking Office *(tel: 223 3762)*.

Train timetables are published in the bi-monthly *Thomas Cook Overseas Timetable*, available from Thomas Cook in the UK (tel: 01733 503571) or Forsyth Travel Library Inc. in the US, (tel: 800–367–7894).

By road

The main overland entry to Thailand consists of three road crossings on the Thai–Malaysian border in Songkhla, Yala and Narathiwat provinces. VIP and air-conditioned buses leave from Singapore, Kuala Lumpur, Butterworth and many intermediate destinations in Malaysia. Recently a road connection to Laos opened via the Friendship Bridge.

By sea

There are no regular boat connections with Thailand. Cargo boats calling at Bangkok's Klong Toey port sometimes have passenger cabins. Luxury cruise ships periodically visit Pattaya.

CAMPING

Some of the islands, including Ko Samet, and a few national parks now have camping facilities. However, camping is not recommended either by the tourist authorities or by the police.

CHILDREN

Children under 10, and less than 1m tall, can travel free on trains and buses, but are not guaranteed a seat (ie they must travel on their parents' knees if no seats are available). On internal flights, Thai Airways International offers a 50 per cent discount to children under 12 and a 90 per cent discount for those under 2, although you will be required to bring some form of identification.

As a rule children are extremely well treated throughout the country. Most big hotels have cots, and baby food and nappies are available. For advice over inoculations and medical care, contact your local doctor well before departure.

CLIMATE

Thailand has two distinct climates: tropical in most parts of the country and tropical monsoon in the southern region. The so-called hot season lasts from March to May and is the least pleasant time to visit. The rainy season, from June to October has hot heavy days punctuated by sudden downpours. The cool season, which is the most ideal and

A sign prohibiting topless bathing

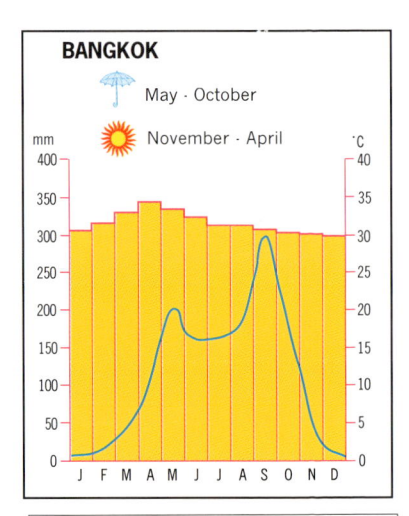

BANGKOK

May - October
November - April

Weather Chart Conversion
25.4mm = 1 inch
°F = 1.8 × °C + 32

popular time to visit, lasts from November to February.

Average temperatures in Bangkok are about 27°C (81°F), ranging from 29°C (84°F) in the hottest month of April to 25°C (77°F) in December. In the north the climate is more temperate with cool-season temperatures falling to as low as 6°C (48°F).

CLOTHING

Light, loose cotton clothing is best suited for the climate. Avoid man-made fibres but bring a sweater if you intend to visit the mountainous areas of the north or northeast during the cool season. Most items of clothing can be purchased easily in Bangkok.

CRIME

Crime is on the increase in Thailand. Carry only limited amounts of cash on

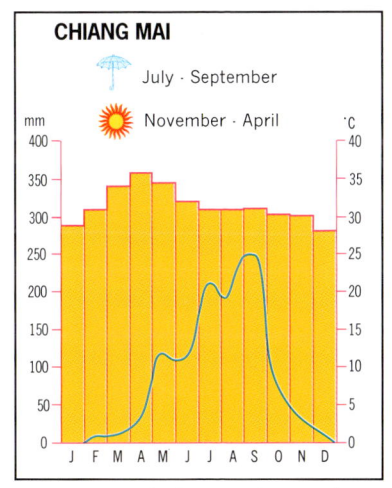

CHIANG MAI

July · September
November · April

PHUKET

May · October
December · March

your person and what you do carry, keep in different pockets. Use a money belt for your passport and credit cards. If you deposit valuables in a hotel safe, get an official receipt in English and an official stamp noting the precise contents. Beware pickpockets and thieves who use razor blades. They are gone before you even know you have lost anything.

If something is stolen, report the theft immediately to the tourist police and, if you intend to claim on insurance, get an official document. For Thomas Cook travellers' cheque loss or theft contact the emergency number on page 179.

Finally, never accept gifts of sweets and drinks on trains or buses. There have been several cases in which passengers have been drugged and robbed and the tourist authorities recently issued warnings.

CUSTOMS REGULATIONS

All narcotics (including cannabis, opium, cocaine, morphine and heroin), obscene literature, pictures and articles, and firearms are prohibited. It would be advisable to fully label all tablets and first aid, and to carry proof of purchase with you at all times.

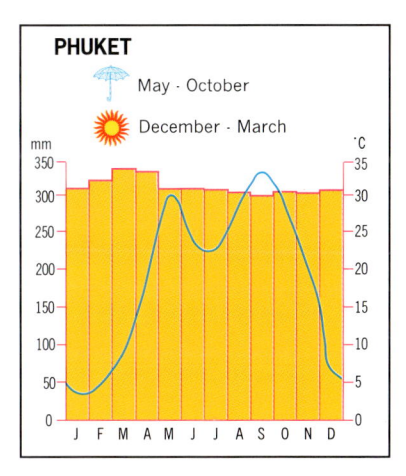

A reasonable amount of clothing for personal use is allowed, along with a litre of spirits and up to 200 cigarettes.

There is no restriction on the import of foreign currency but amounts over the equivalent of US$10,000 must be declared. Leaving via a neighbouring nation will allow you to take bt500,000 out of Thailand; you can only take bt50,000 out of Thailand otherwise.

Buddha images and antiques cannot be taken out of the country without express permission. Some may even need an export licence from the government Fine Arts Department. Shops should be able to arrange this for you.

DISABILITIES, TRAVELLERS WITH

Few special facilities exist for travellers with disabilities in Thailand. Lift services are, however, available in all the major hotels and wheelchairs are available at Don Muang International Airport and at all the local airports.

Jeep for hire, Pattaya

The Tourist Authority of Thailand (TAT) or Thai embassies abroad should be able to provide information prior to arrival. There is also an Association for the Disabled in Bangkok *(tel: 463 5929)*.

DRIVING

Cars and jeeps can be hired by anyone aged over 21 (age limits vary) who possesses a valid driving licence. Those without a driving knowledge of Asia would be unwise to do so. Vehicles drive on the left (generally) but the size of the vehicle is the final arbiter. Trucks often take up the whole of the road and it is up to you to get out of the way. The speed limit is 60kmh in towns, 80kmh on highways and 100kmh on expressways, although few people take much notice. Finally, never drive at night.

Petrol and oil are readily available and at prices similar to those in Europe. Most rental firms also operate rescue services. Road signs are generally to the international standard, although directions in the remote provinces may be written exclusively in Thai script.

Make sure you have insurance, as many of the smaller hire companies do not include it. See 'Insurance', page 181. You may also be required to pay a deposit equal to the estimated cost of the rental.

Avis and Hertz both rent cars and jeeps, and will also be able to arrange chauffeur-driven vehicles.

Avis
Bangkok, *Bangkok International Airport (tel: 255 5300)*.
Chiang Mai, *Chiang Mai Airport (tel: 221 316)*.
Ko Samui, *Imperial Samui Hotel (tel: 421 390)*.
Phuket, *opposite Phuket Airport (tel: 327 358)*.

Hertz
Bangkok, *2563 Titr-Ur Thai Building, 9th Floor, Ramkhamhaeng Road (tel: 722 6161)*.
Chiang Mai, *90 Sridonchoi Road (tel: 270 184)*.
Phuket, *Phuket Airport (tel: 217 190)*.
For details of motorbikes see page 132.

DRUGS

Thailand is one of the world's major distribution centres for opium and heroin brought in from the Golden Triangle. Never accept a package from any stranger, whoever they may claim to be, and never consider smuggling drugs into or out of the country. Just before and after going through customs control check rucksacks and bags, and let

Two-seater motorbikes are available for hire

officials see you doing it! Possession or consumption is an extremely serious offence, punishable by life imprisonment or by the death sentence.

ELECTRICITY
The standard electric current is 220 volts, 50 cycles AC, although different kinds of socket are used around the country. Most hotels have a point for shavers and some have 110 volt sockets. It is best, however, to bring an adaptor.

EMBASSIES AND CONSULATES
The following is an abbreviated list of embassies and consulates in Bangkok. For a full list, see the *Yellow Pages* telephone directory.
Australia
37 Sathorn Tai Road (tel: 287 2680).
Canada
11th & 12th Floor Boonmiter Building, 138 Silom Road (tel: 238 4452).
New Zealand
93 Wireless (Witthayu) Road (tel: 251 8165).
Republic of Ireland
United Flour Mills Building, 11th Floor, 205 Ratchawongse Road (tel: 223 0876).
UK
1031 Wireless (Witthayu) Road (tel: 253 0191).
United States
95 Wireless (Witthayu) Road (tel: 252 5040 or 252 5171).

EMERGENCY TELEPHONE NUMBERS
Ambulance: *(tel: 252 2171)*.
Fire: *(tel: 199)*.
Highway Police: *(tel: 693 in emergencies, or 245 7809)*.
Police Emergencies: *(tel: 191)*.
Tourist Police: *(tel: 1699 in emergencies)*.
Tourist Assistance Centre: *(tel: 281 5051 or 282 8129)*.

Thomas Cook travellers' cheque loss or theft: *(tel: Peterborough, UK on +44 1733 318950 – reverse charges)* or *(tel: Melbourne, Australia +61 3696 2952 – reverse charges)*.
MasterCard card loss or theft: *(tel: 001–800–11887– 0663, toll free)*.

Emergency local assistance can also be obtained from Thomas Cook Travellers' Cheques representative office 8th floor, Bank of Asia Building, 191 South Sathorn Road, Yannawa,

Please observe the signs, no matter how odd

Bangkok and from Turismo Thai, see page 190.

ETIQUETTE
Never touch a monk or criticise the monarchy. Never go nude bathing and always wear reasonable clothes when visiting a temple. Photography is prohibited at Don Muang International Airport and at any military installation.

HEALTH
No inoculations or vaccinations are required unless you are coming from or passing through contaminated areas.

Colourful and traditional costumes

Yellow fever vaccinations may be required if arriving from an endemic country. However, most doctors advise a boost of typhoid/cholera as well as malaria tablets and an optional hepatitis injection. Ask your doctor for advice.

You are also advised to bring a small first-aid pack including needles, plasters and iodine.

Never drink the tap water (bottled and boiled water is widely available), beware heat exposure (wear a hat) and most of all take precautions against venereal and other infectious diseases. Remember that Thailand is currently said to have more than 500,000 known HIV-positive cases.

All the main hospitals treat urgent medical problems 24 hours a day, although you are expected to pay for treatment on the spot. Provincial towns also have reasonably equipped hospitals, elsewhere facilities are rudimentary.

The following hospitals in Bangkok have emergency departments:
Bangkok Adventist Hospital (24-hour emergency) *430 Phitsanulok Road (tel: 281 1422 or 282 1100).*
Bangkok General Hospital,
2 Soi Soonwichai, 7 New Phetchaburi Road (tel: 318 0066).
Police Central,
492/1 Ratchadamri Road, Pathumwan (tel: 252 8111).
St Louis Hospital,
215 South Sathorn Tai Road (tel: 212 0033).
Bangkok also has extremely proficient dentists at low prices.

HITCH-HIKING
Hitch-hiking is possible in many of the rural areas but is considered unsafe. Women should never attempt to hitch a lift alone.

INSURANCE

Insurance is strongly recommended and should cover you for lost or stolen cash and credit cards and guarantee a return ticket in case of emergency. Make sure that you get special cover if items like cameras exceed the individual limit. Report lost or stolen items to the tourist police for an officially stamped statement. Without it, insurance firms can refuse to pay claims money.

If you hire a car, collision insurance (collision damage waiver or CDW), is normally offered by the hirer, and is usually compulsory. Check with your own motor insurers if your normal policy covers you. If not, CDW is payable locally and may be as much as 50 per cent of the hiring fee. Neither CDW nor your personal travel insurance will protect you for liability arising out of an accident in a hire car if you damage another vehicle or injure someone. If you are likely to hire a car in Thailand, obtain such extra cover from your travel agent or other insurer before departure.

LANGUAGE

Thai is a highly complex language with 44 consonants, 38 vowels and five different tones. Few tourists will have the chance to learn it in a limited period, but a few words will prove useful. Men use the word *Krap* at the end of certain sentences, women the work *Ka*; these are indicated by (m) and (f) below.

Numbers

0	Soon	13	Sip–sam
1	Nung	14	Sip–see
2	Song	15	Sip–ha
3	Sam	16	Sip–hok
4	See	17	Sip–jet
5	Ha	18	Sip–baet
6	Hok	19	Sip–goa
7	Jet	20	Yee–sip
8	Baet	21	Yee–sip–et
9	Gao	30	Sam–sip
10	Sip	100	Nung roi
11	Sip–et	1,000	Nung pan
12	Sip–song	10,000	Nung meun

Basic phrases
Thank you Kop khun krap(m)/ka(f)
Hello/goodbye Sawatdee krap(m)/ka(f)
Yes Chai or krap(m)/ka(f)
No Mai
How are you? Sabai dee ru ?
I'm fine Sabai dee
I'm not well Mai sabai krap(m)/ka(f)
Never mind Mai pen rai

The fine face of a Phang Nga fisherman

I understand Kao chai
I don't understand Mai kao chai
Please speak slowly Prot puut cha–cha
I'm sorry Sia chai
Excuse me Kor thot
Very good Dee mak
No good Mai dee
Cheap Tuk
Too expensive Peng pai
Too small Lek pai
Too big Yai pai
A little Nid noi

Questions
What is your name? Khun chu arai?
My name is... Pom chu(male)
  Chan chu (female)
How old are you? Ayu taorai ?
I am (ten) years old Ayu (sip) pi
Do you have...? Mi may...?
Where is the hotel...? Rongreem yu tinnay...?
What is this in Thai? Thai riak wa arai?
How much does this cost? Nee taorai?

Directions
Where are you going? Pai nai
I'm going to... Ja pai...
Where is the...? Yu tii nai...?
Turn right Lieo khwa
Turn left Lieo sai
Straight on Trong pai
Stop here Jop tinni

Places
Airport Sanambin
Bank Tanakaan
Bathroom Hong nam
Beach Hat
Bus station Sa-tanee rot meh
Embassy Sa-tantoot
Hospital Rong payabaan
Hotel Rong reem
Island Ko

Market Talaht
Police station Satanee tamruat
Police Tamruat
Post office Prai-sanee
Railway station Satanee rot fai
Restaurant Raan ahaan
River Maenam
Street Thanon
Sidestreet/lane Soi
Train Rot fai
Town Meung

Transport
Boat Reuah
Bus Rot meh
Car Rot keng
Dangerous Andalay
Motorbike Rot motorcye
Please drive slowly Prot put cha cha
Petrol Naman
I have no petrol Naman mot leo
It doesn't work Mai tit
Garage Rong rot
Help Chuay pom (M)/diichan (F)

Time
Today Wan nee
Tomorrow Proong nee
Yesterday Meua wan nee
This week Atit ni
Next week Atit na
This month Deuan ni
Next month Deuan na
Now Diao nee
Later Tee lang
Minute Na tee
Hour Chua mong
How many hours? Kee chua mong?

Food
Beef Neua
Chicken Gai
Duck Phet
Fish Pla
Pork Moo

Prawns Kung
Spicy soup Tom yam
Fried noodles Mi crob
Rice Khao
Fried rice Khao pat
Fried chicken rice Khao pat gai
Curry Kaeng
Seafood Aahaan thaleh
Fried fish Pla tot
Sweet-and-sour fish Pla priaw wan
Steamed fish Pla neung
Steamed crab (claws) (Kam) pu nung
Mixed vegetables Pat Pak
Thai spicy salad Yam
Lobster Gung yai
Eggs Khai
Plain omelette Khai jiao
Chilli Phrik
Black pepper Phrik thai
Salt Kleua
Fish sauce Nam pla

Ordering food
Hot (spicy) Pet
Not hot Mai pet
Delicious Aroy
I can't eat... Kin... mai dai
I'm vegetarian Kin jeh

Fruit
Banana Kluai
Coconut Maphrao-on
Lime Manao
Mango Ma muang
Orange Som
Papaya Malako
Pineapple Sapparot
Watermelon Taeng moh

Drink
Water Nam
A glass of water? Nam plao?
Tea Chaa
Coffee Cafee
No sugar Mai sai nam-taan

LOST PROPERTY

If you lose something on a bus or train, make enquiries at the local station. Most hotels and restaurants will also keep lost property for a limited period of time. Outside that, contact the nearest tourist police station.

MAPS

Bartholomew, Macmillan, GeoCenter and Nelles all produce good countrywide maps of Thailand. For Bangkok try to get a map with all bus routes marked as well as the *soi* (sidestreet) numbers. The *Tour 'n Guide Map*, published by SK Thaveepholcharoen, is reliable and can be purchased at most hotels and book shops. Most of the free magazines distributed in the hotels also have reasonable maps.

Free local maps are available from tourist offices and many guest houses. While the standard of cartography is not high, these maps are often very useful sources of tourist information.

MEASUREMENTS AND SIZES

Almost everything in Thailand is metric. All distances are measured in kilometres, weights in kilos and liquids in litres. Thailand also has one or two of its own terms. Thus a *sok* is 0.5m, a *wah* is 2m, and a *rai* is 1,600sq km.

MEDIA

Thailand has two English-language newspapers, the *Bangkok Post* and *The Nation,* which provide local and international news and can be purchased in most big hotels and news stalls. The *Asian Wall Street Journal,* the *International Herald Tribune, Time Magazine* and *Newsweek* are also widely available.

Thailand also has some 400 radio stations broadcasting from Bangkok and

Men's Suits
UK		36	38	40	42	44	46	48
Rest of Europe	46	48	50	52	54	56	58
US		36	38	40	42	44	46	48

Dress Sizes
UK		8	10	12	14	16	18
France	36	38	40	42	44	46
Italy	38	40	42	44	46	48
Rest of Europe	34	36	38	40	42	44
US		6	8	10	12	14	16

Men's Shirts
UK	14	14.5	15	15.5	16	16.5	17
Rest of Europe	36	37	38	39/40	41	42	43
US	14	14.5	15	15.5	16	16.5	17

Men's Shoes
UK	7	7.5	8.5	9.5	10.5	11
Rest of Europe	41	42	43	44	45	46
US	8	8.5	9.5	10.5	11.5	12

Women's Shoes
UK	4.5	5	5.5	6	6.5	7
Rest of Europe	38	38	39	39	40	41
US	6	6.5	7	7.5	8	8.5

Conversion Table
FROM	TO	MULTIPLY BY
Inches	Centimetres	2.54
Feet	Metres	0.3048
Yards	Metres	0.9144
Miles	Kilometres	1.6090
Acres	Hectares	0.4047
Gallons	Litres	4.5460
Ounces	Grams	28.35
Pounds	Grams	453.6
Pounds	Kilograms	0.4536
Tons	Tonnes	1.0160

To convert back, for example from centimetres to inches, divide by the number in the third column.

the provinces. Several stations have English-language broadcasts, listed in the English-language newspapers.

Satellite television is now available in many hotels.

MONEY MATTERS

The Thai currency is denominated in *baht* and each *baht* in turn is divided into 100 *satang*. Thai notes consist of bt1,000 (orange and grey), bt500 (purple), bt100 (red), bt50 (blue), bt20 (green) and bt10 (brown). Thai coins are 25 *satang*, 50 *satang*, 1 *baht*, 5 *baht* and 10 *baht*. As a rule take small notes, as in many places it can be hard getting change for a 500 baht note.

The Thai *baht* is freely interchangeable with most other currencies, although outside Bangkok exchange banks are fewer and further between. Rates are generally advertised outside the bank or in the local newspaper.

Bank services

Local and foreign banks provide standard services nationwide. The large towns and cities tend to have more reliable opening times. They are open Monday to Friday, from 8.30am to 3.30pm, except on public and bank holidays.

Bank currency exchange offices generally operate from 8am to 9pm daily, including holidays, although quite often they have an annoying tendency to be closed when you actually need them.

Cheques and credit cards

Thomas Cook traveller's cheques, denominated in US dollars, are accepted in denominated in US dollars, are accepted in banks and authorized bureaux de change.

Outside of Bangkok the major hotels will happily accept your traveller's cheques, but the smaller hotels and most of the

To do what, we wonder?

banks probably will not be able to do so.

Major international credit and charge cards, such as American Express, Diners Club, Carte Blanche, MasterCard and Visa are accepted by major banks, restaurants, hotels and shops.

If you need to transfer money quickly, you can use the *MoneyGram*[SM] Money Transfer service. Just take some form of identification with you and you will be able to send or receive money in minutes from over 100 countries around the world. For more details, go to your nearest Thomas Cook location, or if you are in the UK call Freephone 0800 897198.

Banks in Bangkok

Bangkok Bank Ltd, *333 Silom Road (tel: 231 4333)*.
Citibank, *127 Sathorn Road (tel: 213 2441)*.
Hong Kong and Shanghai Banking Corporation, *63 Silom Road (tel: 233 1904)*.
Siam Commercial Bank, *1060 Phetchaburi Road (tel: 256 1121)*.
Standard Chartered Bank, *Dusit Thani Building, 946 Rama IV Road (tel: 234 0821)*.
Thai Farmers' Bank, *400 Phahon Yothin Road (tel: 270 1122/fax: 273 2226)*.

NATIONAL HOLIDAYS

Thai public holidays vary from year to year according to the lunar calendar so you should always check with the tourist authority or embassy. During Songkran (April), the Thai New Year, hotels in Chiang Mai tend to be booked up weeks ahead and it can be difficult getting transport to and from Bangkok. Restaurants, cinemas and nightclubs generally remain open.

1 January	New Year's Day
Late January	Chinese New Year's Day
Early March	Makha Bucha Day
6 April	Chakri Day
Mid-April	Songkran Day
1 May	National Labour Day
5 May	Coronation Day
Late April/early May	Royal Ploughing Ceremony
May–June	Visakha Puja Day
Late July	Asalha Puja Day
Late July	Khao Phansa
12 August	The Queen's Birthday
23 October	Chulalongkorn Day
5 December	The King's Birthday
10 December	Constitution Day
31 December	New Year's Eve

OPENING HOURS

Most commercial organisations in Bangkok operate a five-day week. Government offices are open Monday to Friday from 8.30am to 4.30pm (some close for 1 hour for lunch) and banks from 8.30am to 3.30pm. Supermarkets and department stores are generally open daily from 10am to 7pm.

Museums normally open from Wednesday to Sunday, being closed on Monday and Tuesday. It is well worth checking first.

ORGANISED TOURS

Tour operators round the world offer a wide choice of package tours to Thailand. These can range from three-day trips (as part of a three-centre tour taking in Hong Kong and Singapore) to 30 days, and include all air transport, transfers, accommodation and sightseeing. Thomas Cook, Abercrombie and Kent, Jetset Tours and Trailfinders are all rated among the leaders.

Local organised tours can also be arranged for almost any and every destination. Make sure you use a reputable organisation. Unauthorised guides and people who approach you on the streets are to be avoided at all costs.

The following agents in Bangkok are recommended by the Tourist Authority of Thailand (TAT).

World Travel Service, Thomas Cook Holidays overseas representative, *1053 Charoen Krung Road (tel: 233 5900).*

Diethelm Travel, *140/1 Wireless Road (tel: 255 9150).*

Overseas International Travel Service, *21st Floor, Rajathevee Tower, 77/283 Phayathai Road (tel: 653 9050).*

Sonne Tour, *3/233 Petchburi, Soi 15, Petchburi Road (tel: 653 7330).*

Ultima Travel, *Judis Tower, 21/53, 3rd Floor Soi 19, Petchburi Road (tel: 254 6078).*

PHARMACIES

Pharmacies are found in all the main towns. They sell almost everything that a normal pharmacy at home does, from medicinal drugs to contraceptives, and everything to do with personal hygiene. Prescriptions are not generally needed for medicinal drugs, but they are often sold under different brands, so bring the generic name. Always check the expiry dates before purchasing.

PHOTOGRAPHY

Film is widely available in Thailand although, just to be sure, most visitors prefer to bring film with them. Keen photographers should also bring a polarising lens, to reduce the glare, and bags of silicate chips, to stop moisture getting into the camera.

Most international film manufacturers have local photofinishing laboratories at marginally cheaper rates than back home.

PLACES OF WORSHIP

Christian churches are found in Bangkok and several provincial capitals. Services are mainly in Thai, with occasional services in English, French or German.

Below is a list of churches in Bangkok:
Assumption Cathedral (Roman Catholic), *23 Oriental Avenue (tel: 233 7120).*
Christ Church, *11 Convent Road (tel: 233 8525 or 234 3634).*
Holy Redeemer Catholic Church, *123/19 Soi Raum Rudee, Wireless (Witthayu) Road (tel: 256 6305).*
The Evangelical Church, *end of Soi 10, Sukhumvit Road (tel: 251 9539).*

POLICE

In case of trouble, contact the tourist police. They generally speak English and can be recognised by their badges. The main office is in **Bangkok** *(tel: 1699 in emergencies, or 652 1721)*. The tourist police also have offices in **Chiang Mai** *(tel: 248 130)*, **Hat Yai** *(tel: 246 733)*, **Kanchana Buri** *(tel: 512 795)*, **Pattaya** *(tel: 425 937)*, **Phuket** *(tel: 429 271)* and **Surat Thani** *(tel: 421 489 or 421 441)*.

POST OFFICES

Almost every town has a post office which will dispatch cards and letters. Big towns also have poste restante offices which receive mail from abroad and have international telephone and fax services.

Airmail generally takes five or six days to reach Europe and eight or nine days to the United States. Packages can also be sent home by air or ship, although you will have to present the contents for inspection at the customs window.

The General Post Office (GPO) has its head office on Charoen Krung Road in Bangkok and is open from 8am to 8pm Monday to Friday and 9am to 1pm Saturday, Sunday and public holidays. Outside Bangkok offices are open from 8.30am to 4.30pm on Monday to Friday and from 9am–1pm on Saturday.

Cathedral of the Assumption, Bangkok

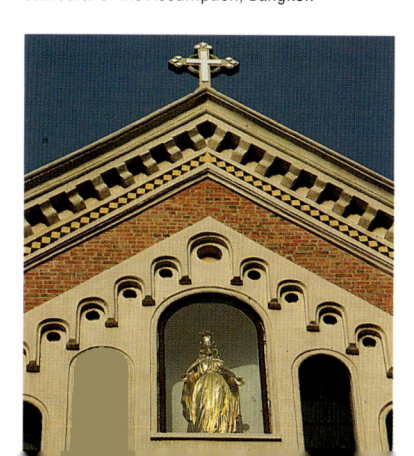

PUBLIC TRANSPORT

Air
Thai Airways International operates daily flights between Bangkok and virtually every major town in Thailand. Bangkok Airways also has flights from Bangkok to Ko Samui and Hua Hin and from Phuket to Ko Samui.

Reservations can be made through any authorised Thai Inter Travel Agent. Thai Airways International's main office is on *6 Lan Luang Road (tel: 280 0060)*. Book well in advance at all times and especially over local holidays when seats are taken up months in advance.

The local airport tax is bt30. Planes leave from Don Muang Domestic Airport next to the international terminal.

Bus
Buses offer a fast, if somewhat harrowing, means of transport to most places. VIP tour coaches offer greater comfort but at a slightly higher cost. Normal public buses are designed for Thais, not foreigners, and leg room is limited.

A number of private companies also run air-conditioned and VIP coaches to major tourist destinations. Bangkok has the following public bus terminals.
Northern and Northeastern Bus Terminal. *Phahon Yothin Road (tel: 272 5242)*.
Southern Bus Terminal. *Phra Pinklao Road, Thonburi (tel: 434 5557)*.
Eastern Bus Terminal. *Sukhumvit Road (tel: 392 9227 or 391 9829)*.

Rail
A slow, but efficient, rail system links major northern, northeastern and southern towns with the capital. Trains from Bangkok take 12 hours to Chiang Mai, 11 hours to Nong Khai and 12 hours to Surat Thani (the jump-off point for Ko Samui). Local trains generally have three classes. On longer trips you can also book a sleeper. Try to make reservations several days before you travel.

Efficient trains cover vast distances in Thailand; the main station in Bangkok is Hualamphong

The main railway station in Bangkok is Hualamphong on *Rama IV Road (tel: 223 7010 or 223 7020)* which also has a booking office for advance reservations. Most travel agents will also book train tickets at a small surcharge.

The *Visit Thailand Rail Pass* is available to visitors with international passports for travel on all State Railway of Thailand trains. Obtainable from advance booking office at Bangkok, Hualumphong and other major stations, but check how worthwhile it will be.

Details of local rail, bus and ferry services are shown in the *Thomas Cook Overseas Timetable* which is available from Thomas Cook branches in the UK or by telephoning (01733) 503571.

River
Thailand has an extensive network of waterways. In Bangkok, ferry services are the best way to avoid the traffic. The public Chao Phraya express boat costs about bt10 and the private long-tailed boats about bt350 an hour.

Local transport

Meter taxis, *tuk tuks* (three-wheeled scooters), *songthaews* (pick-up trucks) and tricycles operate in various parts of Thailand and at most times of day or night. To avoid problems, get your hotel to write your destination down in Thai and present it to the driver. Always agree a price before starting and remember to bargain. If one sounds too expensive, wait for another.

Big hotels also run their own taxis and limousines that can be rented by the hour or by the day. These are considerably more expensive, but generally have the advantage of an English-speaking driver.

Local buses

Buses around Bangkok are either red, blue or green and have numbers on them. They are all very cheap and frequent. They leave extremely regularly and serve all parts of the city. More comfortable and less crowded air-conditioned buses also operate, costing slightly more. To work out which bus to take, it is essential to buy a map marked with bus routes.

STUDENT AND YOUTH TRAVEL

Student discounts are occasionally offered on air tickets but not on trains or buses. Some museums also offer discounts, although you will need identification. There are no official youth hostels in Thailand, but the YMCA and YWCA in Bangkok offer good standards and services.
YMCA *Collins International House, 27 Sathorn Tai Road (tel: 287 2727/ fax: 287 1966).*

TELEPHONES

Local and international telephone services are available in most hotels and post offices. Do not expect perfection. Because of the time differences it can be difficult getting a line to Europe in the late afternoon.

Local phone boxes take small bt1 coins or bt5 coins which should be inserted before you dial the number.

The Thomas Cook Traveltalk card is an international pre-paid telephone card supported by 24-hour multi-lingual customer service. Available from Thomas Cook branches in the UK in £10 and £20 denominations, the card can be re-charged by calling the customer service unit and quoting your credit card number.

Local directory assistance	13
Domestic long distance	101
International assistance	100
International codes:	
Australia	61
Canada	1
Ireland	353
New Zealand	64
UK	44
USA	1

TIME

Time in Thailand is 7 hours ahead of Greenwich Mean Time (GMT). That means when it is noon in Bangkok, it is 5am in London, midnight in New York and 3pm in Sydney.

TIPPING

Tipping, once hardly expected, is increasingly on the uptake. In some international restaurants a 10 per cent service charge is included. In other big restaurants tip in the region of 5 to 10 per cent – and in smaller restaurants a bt20 note is normally adequate. It is not necessary to tip taxi drivers or cinema attendants.

TOILETS

In the cities and in the tourist-visited areas, there are normally sit-down loos. Outside that in the provinces, it's squat loos and in the really far flung provinces, a rice paddy.

If you are caught short, go into a shop or restaurant and ask for the *hong nam* (bathroom) and to be on the safe side, always bring a toilet roll with you on your travels.

TOURIST OFFICES

Tourist information is available at TAT offices throughout Thailand and in certain countries abroad. The officials are generally extremely helpful and speak English. They will distribute maps, brochures and useful information on tours, shopping, dining and, crucially, accommodation.

Bangkok
Head Office, *Ratchadamnoen, Nok Avenue (tel: 282 1143)*.
New Office, *372 Bamrung Muang Road (tel: 226 0075)*.
Chiang Mai
105/1 Chiang Mai-Lamphun Road (tel: 248 604/fax: 248 605).
Hat Yai
1/1 Soi 2 Niphat Uthit 3 Road (tel: 243 747 or 231 055).
Kanchana Buri
Saeng Chuto Road (tel: 511 200).
Nakhon Ratchasima
2102/2104 Mittraphap Road (tel: 213 666/fax: 213 667).
Pattaya
382/1 Mu 10 Chaihat Road (tel: 427 667).

Phitsanulok
209/7–8 Surasi Trade Centre, Boromtrailokanat Road (tel: 252 742).
Phuket
73/75 Phuket Road (tel: 212 213 or 211 036/fax: 213 582).
Suratthani
5 Talat Mai Road, Ban Don (tel: 281 828).
Ubon Ratchathani
264/1 Khaun Thani Road (tel: 243 770).

Thomas Cook offices
Turismo Thai is the Thomas Cook Worldwide licensee in Thailand. The main branch is at:
Turismo Thai Building, *511 Soi 6, Sri Ayutthaya Road, Bangkok 10400 (tel: 642 4504/5; fax: 246 3993)*.

Besides offering a full leisure travel service they also organise airport transfers, rail tickets and reservations, car hire and general information and assistance.

They can provide emergency assistance in the event of loss or theft of Thomas Cook traveller's cheques.

VALETING/LAUNDRY

Most hotels will offer their guests a fast and efficient laundry service. Most items are returned the same day if they are given in before 9am and, if you are in a real hurry, they can be laundered and returned in as little as four hours. Prices will vary depending on the establishment, but are invariably cheaper than in Western hotels.

WHAT TO TAKE

A good first-aid kit, a valid passport, sufficient travellers' cheques, insurance, sunglasses, a sun hat and loose cotton clothing are all items that should not be left at home. Finally a thorough read of this travel guide will help prepare you for what will be an experience of a lifetime.

INDEX

A
accommodation 170–3
air transport 188
Ancient City 66
Ang Sila 106
Ang Thong Marine Park 124
Ao Phranang 131
arriving 174–5
Ayutthaya 64–5

B
Ban Chiang 101
Ban Doi Pui 80
Ban Ko Noi 93
Ban Ruammit 87
Ban Sop Ruak 88
Ban Taba 129
Bang Pa-in 65
Bang Saen 22, 103, 106
Bangkok 44–73
 bars and restaurants 32–3
 Celestial Residence 46–7
 Chao Phraya river 28–9, 62–3
 children's attractions 48, 49, 53, 156
 China Town 24–5, 48
 churches 25, 29, 31, 187
 Dusit Zoo 48, 49, 156
 entertainment 148
 festivals 154
 Grand Palace 5, 12, 27, 44, 50–1
 main attractions 46–57
 markets 25, 26, 33, 53
 National Museum 54–5
 nearby sights 64–9, 72–3
 Oriental Hotel 26
 restaurants 168
 shopping 28, 56, 142–3
 temples 5, 13, 25, 26–31, 44, 51, 58–9, 64–5
 Thonburi district 30–1, 44
 tours 24–35
 Vimanmek 46–7
banks 185
bars and pubs 146–9
bird watching 130–1
boxing 33, 160
Buddhism 60–1
Buddhist meditation 131
bull fighting 116
Buri Ram 94
buses 188, 189

C
camping 175–6
car hire 178
caving 131
Cha-am 119
Chaiya 125
Chantha Buri 106–7
Chao Phraya river 8, 28–9, 62–3
Chiang Khan 96
Chiang Mai 22, 74–9, 137
 Chiang Mai Zoo 75, 156
 children's attractions 156
 entertainment 148–9
 environs 80–3, 86–93
 flower festival 154
 history 74–5
 markets 37, 39
 restaurants 168–9
 shopping 143
 temples 7, 36–9, 78–9, 80, 81, 156
 walking tour 36–7
 walled city tour 38–9
Chiang Rai 86–7, 136, 137
Chiang Saen 89
children 156–7, 176
Chon Buri 103, 107
Chung Kai War Cemetery 35
cinemas 147, 148, 149
climate 176
climbing 132
clothing 21, 176
coral islands 104
crime 176–7
Crocodile Farm 66–7
culture 12–13
customs regulations 177

D
Damnoen Saduak 67
deep-sea fishing 162
disabilities, travellers with 177–8
discothèques 147, 148, 149
Doi Inthanon 8, 80, 132, 133
Doi Suthep Temple 80, 81, 156
driving 178
drugs 88, 177, 178–9

E
Eastern Gulf 102–9
electricity 179
elephants 82–3, 87, 100, 104, 156
Emerald Buddha 51
embassies and consulates 179
entertainment 146–55
entry formalities 174
Erawan National Park 69
etiquette 180

F
festivals 154–5
fighting fish 160
fitness centres 158
food and drink 109, 122, 126–7, 164–9, 167, 171, 180

G
gems 106–7
geography 8–9
Golden Triangle 84, 88–9, 130, 178
golf 159
greetings 14, 15
Gulf of Thailand 22

H
Hat Yai 116
health 180
hilltribes 84–5, 87
history 6–7
hitch-hiking 180
horse racing 159
hospitals 180
hotels 147, 170–3
Hua Hin 118–19

I
insurance 178, 181
island hopping 132
Issan 22, 98–9

J
Jeath War Museum 35

K
Kaeng Khut Khu Rapids 96
Kanchana Buri 34, 68–9, 136
Karon/Kata 113
Khao Yai National Park 69, 94, 130, 132, 133
Khawowsinrin 101
Khmers, the 95
Khu Khut Waterbird Sanc 130
Khwae (Kwai) Bridge and River 34–5, 35, 68, 155
Khwae Noi River 136
kite-flying 156, 160
Ko Chang 22, 108
Ko Kradat 108
Ko Lan 104, 156–7
Ko Mak 108
Ko Phai 104
Ko Phangan 124, 132
Ko Samet 22, 108–9, 175
Ko Samui 22, 122–5, 132, 157
Ko Tao 125, 132
Kok river 86–7
Korat 94–5
Krabi 22, 126, 131, 132

L
Lake Songkhla 134
Lampang 80–1
Lamphun 82
language 16, 182–3
Lanna 22
laundry 190
local transport 189
Loei province 96–101, 132
longboat racing 160, 161
Lop Buri 72
lost property 184

M
Mae Chan 87
Mae Hong Son 90–1, 137, 154
Mae Klong river 35
Mae Sa Valley 82, 156
Mae Sai 88–9
Mae Salong 87
Mae Sariang 90
Mae Sot 5
Mae Taeng 82–3
Mai Khao Beach 157
maps 184
 Bangkok 46–7
 Chiang Mai 76–7
 general map of Thailand 15
 Northern Thailand 16–17
 Phuket 111
 Southern Thailand 23
 Thailand within Asia 8
 see also walks section
markets 20, 144–5
massage 161

INDEX

measurements and sizes 184
media 184–5
Mekong river 8, 88, 96, 97
money matters 185
motorbiking 132–3
muay Thai 33, 160
music 13, 147–8

N
Nail Island 114, 115
Nakha Noi Pearl Farm 114, 157
Nakhon Pathom 34, 73
Nakhon Ratchasima 94–5
Nakhon Sawan 8
Nakhon Si Thammarat 125
Nam Tok 34
Nan river 8
Narathiwat 129
national holidays 186
national parks 133
  see also individual parks
Nong Khai 96–7
Northeast Thailand 22, 94–101
Northern Thailand 22, 74–93

O
opening hours 186
opium 88, 89
orchids 83
organised tours 186

P
Pai 90
Pak Thong Chai 94–5
Pansea 113
paragliding 162
Patong 41, 112
Pattani 129
Pattaya 22, 102–4
  children's attractions 156–7
  entertainment 149
  festival 154
  nearby sights 104–9
  restaurants 169
Phang Nga 115, 131, 157
Phanom Rung 95
pharmacies 187
Phi Mai 94
Phi Phi Islands 126–7

photography 187
Phu Kradung 97, 133, 175
Phu Luang National Park 97
Phu Phing Palace 80
Phuket 22, 40, 110–15, 131, 132
  beaches 41, 112–13
  children's attractions 156
  circular trip 40–1
  entertainment 149
  nearby sights 114–15
  restaurants 169
Ping river 8
police 187
politics 10–11
post offices 187
prostitution 150
public transport 188–9

R
rafting 136
railways 188
Rayong 22, 109
religion 12
restaurants 168–9
rice production 8, 9, 70–1
river transport 28–9, 62–3, 188
royalty 120–1

S
Sai Yok National Park 69, 136
sailing 136–7, 162
Sam Roi Yod National Park 119
Sanghkla Buri 69
Sattahip 103
scuba diving 162–3
sea turtles 113
shopping 20, 138–45
Si Racha 103
Si Satchanalai 93
Similan Islands 115, 133
Songkhla 116–17
Soppong 90, 131
Southern Thailand 110–29
sport 158–63
student and youth travel 189
Suan Mokhapalaram 131
Sukhothai 42–3, 92–3
Sungai Kolok 129
Suratthani 125

Surin 94, 100–1, 113
swimming 159

T
Taklang 101
takraw-rattan ballgame 161
Tarutao Marine National
  Park 128, 132, 133
taxis 20, 21
telephones 189
  emergency numbers 179
temples 13, 21, 59
  see also under individual place
tennis 159
Tha Ton 86, 136
Thai drama and dancing 152–3
Thailand Meditation Centre 131
Thale Noi Bird Sanctuary 130
Tham Lot Cave 131
Thomas Cook offices 190
time 189
tipping 171, 189
toilets 190
tourist offices 190
touts 20
travellers' cheques, loss 177
trekking 137
tuk tuks 21

U
Udon Thani 101

V
valeting 190
visa requirements 174

W
walks 24–44
watersports 162
waterways, Bangkok 62–3
wats 13, 21
what to take 190
wildlife 134–5
windsurfing 163
worship, places of 187

Y
Yala 129
Yom river 8

ACKNOWLEDGEMENTS
The Automobile Association wishes to thank the folllowing photographers, libraries and associations for their assistance in the preparation of this book.

Rick Strange was commissioned to take all the pictures for the book except the following.
TIM LOCKE 35 Kanchanaburi Death Railway
PICTURES COLOUR LIBRARY spine
POWERSTOCK PHOTO LIBRARY front and back covers
SPECTRUM COLOUR LIBRARY 76 Food Stall, 147 Signs, 151 Bangkok signs
TOURISM AUTHORITY OF THAILAND 33 Thai Kick Boxing, 55 Ancient Buddha Image, 56 Royal Barges, 67 Damnoen Saduak, 84 Lisiu Hill Tribe, 98 Isaan Folk Dance, 110 Phuket, 120 Queen Sirikit, 123 Samui, 128 Kho Tarutaro, 136 Raft Ride, 140 Souvenirs, 142 Thai Jewellery, 143 Thai Silk, 154 Candle Festival, 155 Pra Festival, 155 Yok Mub Festival, 159 Ball Game, 161 Boat Race, 164 Vegetables, 165 Seafood, 168 Tai food, 175 Thai Airways International, 180 Traditional Costumes.

CONTRIBUTORS
Series adviser: Melissa Shales **Copy editor:** Helen Douglas-Cooper **Indexer:** Marie Lorimer
Thanks also to **Sheila Hawkins** for her updating work on this revised edition